JAMES MERRILL'S POETIC QUEST

Recent Titles in
Contributions to the Study of World Literature

Orienting Masculinity, Orienting Nation: W. Somerset Maugham's Exotic Fiction
Philip Holden

A Matter of Faith: The Fiction of Brian Moore
Robert Sullivan

Samuel Johnson and the Essay
Robert D. Spector

Fighting Evil: Unsung Heroes in the Novels of Graham Greene
Haim Gordon

Pearl S. Buck: A Cultural Bridge Across the Pacific
Kang Liao

A Systems Approach to Literature: Mythopoetics of Chekhov's Four Major Plays
Vera Zubarev

Reflections of Change: Children's Literature Since 1945
Sandra L. Beckett

Nordic Experiences: Exploration of Scandinavian Cultures
Berit I. Brown, editor

Catholic Fiction and Social Reality in Ireland, 1873–1922
James H. Murphy

A Morbid Fascination: White Prose and Politics in Apartheid South Africa
Richard Peck

The Other Mirror: Women's Narrative in Mexico, 1980–1995
Kristine Ibsen, editor

Searching for Recognition: The Promotion of Latin American Literature in the United States
Irene Rostagno

JAMES MERRILL'S POETIC QUEST

Don Adams

Contributions to the Study of World Literature,
Number 81

GREENWOOD PRESS
Westport, Connecticut • London

Library of Congress Cataloging-in-Publication Data

Adams, Don, 1964–
James Merrill's poetic quest / Don Adams.
p. cm. — (Contributions to the study of world literature, ISSN 0738–9345 ; no. 81)
Includes bibliographical references and index.
ISBN 0–313–30250–2 (alk. paper)
1. Merrill, James Ingram—Criticism and interpretation. 2. Quests in literature. I. Title. II. Series.
PS3525.E6645Z515 1997
811′.54—dc20 96–35022

British Library Cataloguing in Publication Data is available.

Library of Congress Catalog Card Number: 96–35022
ISBN: 0–313–30250–2
ISSN: 0738–9345

First published in 1997

Greenwood Press, 88 Post Road West, Westport, CT 06881
An imprint of Greenwood Publishing Group, Inc.

Printed in the United States of America

The paper used in this book complies with the Permanent Paper Standard issued by the National Information Standards Organization (Z39.48–1984).

10 9 8 7 6 5 4 3 2 1

Copyright Acknowledgments

The author and publisher gratefully acknowledge permission for use of the following material:

Adams, Don. "James Merrill's Prism." *The Explicator* 54, no. 3 (1996): 185–87. Reprinted With Permission Of The Helen Dwight Reid Educational Foundation. Published By Heldref Publications 1319 18th St. N.W. Washington, D.C. 20036-1802. Copyright © 1996.

Adams, Don. "Heroes Without Name or Origin: James Merrill's Poetry of Loss." *Notes on Contemporary Literature* (May, 1996). Reprinted by permission of *Notes on Contemporary Literature.*

Reprinted by permission of Farrar, Straus & Giroux, Inc.: Excerpts from *The Complete Poems 1927–1979* by Elizabeth Bishop. Copyright © 1979, 1983 by Alice Helen Methfessel.

Selected lines of poetry by James Merrill in *Selected Poem* (New York: Knopf, 1993); *The Changing Light At Sandover* (New York: Knopf, 1993); *A Scattering of Salts* (New York: Knopf, 1995); *The (Diblos) Notebook* (New York: Atheneum, 1975); *Late Settings* (New York: Atheneum, 1985); *From the First Nine* (New York: Atheneum, 1981). Reprinted by permission of Alfred A. Knopf.

Stevens, Wallace. Extracts from *The Collected Poems* (Random House, 1990); and *The Palm at the End of the Mind* (Random House, 1967). Reprinted by permission of Random House.

Auden, W. H. Extracts from *Collected Poems* (Random House, 1991). Reprinted, in territories other than the British Commonwealth, by permission of Random House.

Auden, W. H. Extracts from *Collected Poems* (Random House, 1991). Reprinted in the British Commonwealth by permission of Faber and Faber Ltd.

Men in their natural lives pursue the concrete no less than the ideal.

Ronald Firbank, *Concerning the Eccentricities of Cardinal Pirelli*

Contents

Acknowledgments

I wish to thank William Matheson and Naomi Lebowitz, both of whom have contributed immeasurably to the writing of this book. I also wish to thank Timothy Materer, and a whole host of others who have helped me along the way: Ben Taylor, David Hadas, Pamela Hadas, Kevin Ray, Rose Passalacqua, Rob Cross, Rich Curtis, Rod Shene, Ted Munter, Christy Auston, Scott Haycock, Lisa Beckstrand, Nancy Hadfield, John Leeds, and Emily Stockard.

I am grateful to James Merrill's poetry editor at Knopf, Harry Smith, and to his literary executors, J. D. McClatchy and Stephen Yenser, for their permission to quote from Merrill's poetry and prose.

Finally, I am indebted to Merrill himself, who responded to my questions with patience and kindness.

Abbreviations

Gaston Bachelard

AD	*Air and Dreams*
WD	*Water and Dreams*
NES	*Le Nouvel Esprit Scientifique*

Elizabeth Bishop

CP	*The Complete Poems*
L	*Letters*

Sigmund Freud

EI	*The Ego and the Id*
FR	*The Freud Reader*
GPT	*General Psychological Theory*
NIL	*New Introductory Lectures on Psycho-Analysis*

Northrop Frye

MD	*The Myth of Deliverance*
SS	*The Secular Scripture*

C. G. Jung

AS	*Alchemical Studies*
PT	*The Psychology of the Transference*

James Merrill

SS	*A Scattering of Salts*
CL	*The Changing Light at Sandover*
DN	*The (Diblos) Notebook*
FFN	*From the First Nine*
LS	*Late Settings*
REC	*Recitative*
SP	*Selected Poems*

Wallace Stevens

NA	*The Necessary Angel*
PEM	*The Palm at the End of the Mind*

Introduction

James Merrill is a difficult poet; at times, extraordinarily so. Yet relatively little critical effort has been directed toward the explication of his difficult poems, much less toward the understanding of his densely layered symbolism. Current critical trends are partially to blame. Mere explication has been made to seem outmoded, yet the very density of symbolic argument in Merrill's best poems works against the critic striving to construe the poet from a highly theoretical perspective. In consequence, critics have tended either to accept the poet's symbolic difficulty as a "given," requiring no special comment or attention, or have been drawn toward the poems that seem most confessional and least dependent on an abstruse symbolism.

This critical neglect of Merrill's symbolic systems has skewed the poet's reputation. Too often he comes off as a mere technical wizard, a brilliant "colorist," in the French manner—the Maurice Ravel of modern American poetry. Or worse, he begins to appear an incorrigible purveyor of "in-jokes," the most talented and successful apologist of the New York homosexual artistic elite. Through current critical eyes, his poems seem more rarefied and effete than they in fact are.

Close attention to the poems' argument reveals a poet who is more intellectually rigorous and morally challenging than it has been common to assume, and more "democratic." Once the poems' symbolism is thoroughly accounted for, the reader will find this poet more accessible and responsible in his poetic argument than perhaps any other contemporary poet of his stature. As with Marcel Proust, Merrill's elitism only seems to exclude the uninitiated, but his work is in fact inclusive of all readers willing to read it carefully and patiently. Again as with Proust, Merrill is compulsive in his attention to detail. What seems offhand and inaccessible comes to seem, on a second, third, and fourth reading, complex and closely argued. No argumentative or symbolic thread is left untucked by this most careful of poets.

What critics have heretofore neglected to provide, and what is so desperately needed with this difficult poet, is a "key" to his multifaceted symbolic system. Merrill is as committed a systematizer as William Butler Yeats or William Blake, but he is more coy than his predecessors. His particular genius is the combining of the confessional poet's autobiographical openness with the mythologizing poet's use of tightly packed symbolism. He weaves the two modes together so seamlessly and with so little apparent effort that it is possible to read some of his most symbolically determined poems as being merely autobiographical in the confessional manner. Conversely, some of the seemingly inaccessible and symbol-laden poems become available to the reader willing to read them in the manner of the confessional poem.

That Merrill's symbolism would lend itself so willingly to the confessional mode seems only natural when we come to understand that this symbolism is based on the psychological and archetypal systems developed and exploited by Sigmund Freud and Carl Jung. The confessional poem is, after all, a product and analog of the therapy session. It is to the work of these pioneering psychologists, then, that we must turn in an attempt to understand Merrill's symbolism. When we do so, we find that Jung's archetypes of psychic individuation are the dominant influence in Merrill's expansive symbolism, but that Freud's skeptical understanding of the constraints of heredity, in all of its manifestations, forms the base of Merrill's belief system. In other words, Merrill relies upon the Jungian model of psychic progress to combat, through poetry, the Freudian skepticism inherent in his own temperament.

Jung's conjoining of the figures of myth with the figures of modern psychology enables the contemporary poet who avails himself of this system to write about his personal experience and psyche in a mythopoeic manner. As Merrill's career progresses, he comes to rely more and more heavily upon the Jungian archetypes of psychic individuation to tell his own life's story. When we come to what is surely his masterpiece, the epic trilogy *The Changing Light at Sandover*, we find that a knowledge of the Jungian system of archetypes is absolutely essential for our understanding of the poem.

In this study, I attempt to read Merrill's poetry through various lenses, but primarily those of Freudian psychology and of Jung's archetypal system. By doing so, I in no way mean to subordinate the poetry to the system from which it draws meaning. Rather, I am attempting to give the poetry as thorough a reading as its complexities require and deserve, while placing it in the context of the literary and intellectual traditions to which it so richly contributes.

1

Time's Damage and Time's Grief: An Introduction to the Quest Model

When James Merrill published his first book of poems in 1951, few would have predicted that he would go on to write the epic poem of his generation, if not of the century. The poems in that first volume, entitled appropriately enough, *First Poems*, were unusually "finished." James Dickey's response was typical. He labeled Merrill the most "graceful" of "the elegants" (97)—that group of young American poets who seemed to derive their tone and manner from the urbane style of W. H. Auden. In his wryly condescending review, Howard Nemerov observed that some of these highly polished "first" poems were good enough to be called second poems (quoted in Howard, 328).

Nemerov is more typical of the poets of his and Merrill's generation, born in the 1920's, in having discovered his mature voice early. Reading poets such as Nemerov, John Ashbery, and Richard Wilbur, we detect relatively little shift in voice from early to late work. From the beginning, their voices have seemed relaxed and assured, and the passing of time has only made them more so. By contrast, Merrill's early voice seems extremely tight and controlled. Not until his third volume, *Water Street*, published in 1962, does he relax into a less obviously mannered style.

When reprinting some of these *First Poems* in the volume *From the First Nine*, Merrill prefaced the selection with an apology:

> These early versions of desire
> We come upon some nights instead of sleep

Blaze tinily, like fire deep
In windowglass far from the fire.

Light years away, their light, their heat
Are almost zero to the sense. We'd fed
Feelings genuine but dead
With language quick but counterfeit. (FFN 11)

The job of the poet is to keep that fire burning. He rekindles a flame in the poem to represent what has been consumed in living. From the very beginning, Merrill has viewed the poet's task as an epic endeavor to save in art what life has squandered. The enormous burden of this task may help to account for the super-polish of these early poems. Behind the highly wrought surface of language and artifice, we sense the desperation of the young poet whose task is beyond him.

Merrill's acknowledged precursor, Marcel Proust, believed that art must save life or else life is lost. Proust's novel is epic not only in proportion but also in spirit: In it and through it, he strives to save his life through art. Dante is Proust's natural precursor in this quest for individualized salvation. This quest is New Testament in spirit. Although Dante's quest has meaning for all Christians, he alone is saved at its completion. It is an egocentric quest for personal salvation.

Dante's forerunner, Virgil, is typical of the Old Testament quest, in which the fate of an entire nation or people hangs in the balance. John Milton's *Paradise Lost* is another example of this Old Testament, public quest. Aeneas and Adam are ciphers, standing for all Romans or all Christians. Comparing Dante's individual elevation in the *Paradiso* to Adam's all-inclusive fall, we see the contrast between the private and public quest.

Proust's quest is even more individual and elitist than Dante's. In Dante, we find a map for salvation that all Christians can follow, at least in spirit, for he has provided materialist metaphors for spiritual growth. But the creative artist alone can follow Proust's map. The rest of humanity has no hope for salvation. They survive at best in the individual and collective memory of others.

From his very earliest poems, Merrill follows Proust in seeking to save life through art. Nevertheless, his poetic method of using materialist metaphors to represent the spiritual quest for salvation is borrowed from Dante and his visionary heirs, Blake and Yeats. Merrill joins the contemporary genre of confessional lyric to the mythical quest-romance narrative form. In Merrill's confessional poems, experience is made to take the shape of the quest for salvation, enlightenment, or deliverance. By joining the confessional lyric to the quest narrative, the poet seeks to reassure us, and himself, that the chaos of quotidian experience may yet lead the willing aspirant to a vision of a wholly ordered world in which all of experience fits into a comprehensive and consoling narrative. The narrative of the quest-romance form is consoling precisely because it is comprehensive, ensuring us that through all of this seeming waste of time, "nothing is lost. Or else: all is translation / And every bit of us is lost in it" (SP 284).

In his poem "A Prism," from his third volume, Merrill takes us down a typically ingenious metaphorical path in which, while imagining himself to be a crystal paperweight, he progresses through the major stages of the quest-romance. By closely examining the poet's use of the quest form in this early lyric, we will prepare ourselves for the much longer and more complicated quest narratives that follow. I quote the poem in full:

> Having lately taken up residence
> In a suite of chambers
> Windless, compact and sunny, ideal
> Lodging for the pituitary gland of Euclid
> If not for a "single gentleman (references),"
> You have grown used to the playful inconveniences,
> The floors that slide from under you helter-skelter,
> Invisible walls put up in mid-
> Stride, leaving you warped for the rest of the day,
> A spoon in water; also that pounce
> Of wild color from corner to page
> Straightway consuming the latter
> Down to your very signature,
> After which there is nothing to do but retire,
> Licking the burn, into—into—
> Look: (Heretofore
> One could have said where one was looking
> In or out. But now it almost—) Look,
> You dreamed of this:
> To fuse in borrowed fires, to drown
> In depths that were not there. You meant
> To rest your bones in a maroon plush box,
> Doze the old vaudeville out, of mind and object,
> Little foreseeing their effect on you,
> Those dagger-eyed insatiate performers
> Who from the first false insight
> To the most recent betrayal of outlook,
> Crystal, hypnotic atom,
> Have held you rapt, the proof, the child
> Wanted by neither. Now and then
> It is given to see clearly. There
> Is what remains of you, a body
> Unshaven, flung on the sofa. Stains of egg
> Harden about the mouth, smoke still

Rises between fingers or from nostrils.
The eyes deflect the stars through years of vacancy.
Your agitation at such moments
Is all too human. You and the stars
Seem both endangered, each
At the other's utter mercy. Yet the gem
Revolves in space, the vision shuttles off.
A toneless waltz glints through the pea-sized funhouse.
The day is breaking someone else's heart. (SP 64–65)

The poem breaks into three parts which parallel the three stages of the archetypal quest: initiating crisis and departure, journey to the underworld, and return home.

The poem begins just prior to the initiating crisis, in the age of innocence, the unselfconscious state of Wordsworthian childhood. The paperweight-lodger is at home in his sunny chambers. It is morning in a new world. As the day proceeds, however, unforeseen complications arise. At first, these are taken to be merely "playful inconveniences." As the sun's rays move through the paperweight prism, floors slide helter-skelter, invisible walls are put up, and, in general, the world grows very complicated.

We have entered the initiating crisis stage of the quest. After having been ravaged by the sun's rays, the paperweight prism experiences an identity crisis, symbolized by the fact that his very signature—the signature on the paper that he is holding down—is no longer refracted into an image on his crystal retina. Without the sun's rays, the crystal prism refracts nothing and contains nothing. The void within reflects a void without. With the loss of the exterior world, the prism finds his inner life also depleted. He is no longer at home in his identity.

Merrill's paperweight prism learns through crisis that appearances are as much reality as one is allowed to know. The prism is bound by its sensations, imprisoned in its perceptions. What the mind can neither perceive nor imagine does not exist. Even this poem is no more than a projection of the prison-house of its creator's mind. The circle of being can only expand or contract, but it can never get outside of itself.

Faced with such knowledge, the paperweight prism considers the alternative to being. To avoid false insights and betrayals of outlook, one can retreat to the coffin of a maroon plush box and put a stop to the vaudeville of mind and object. The prism's dilemma lies in the fact that it knows itself to be neither mind nor object, but something that is indefinite and inexplicable. Whatever this something is, it is not necessary to existence. Self-consciousness is superfluous to being.

In this second section of the poem, beginning with the word "Look," the prism "falls" into the state of self-consciousness. Knowing that he exists, he necessarily realizes that he might not exist. In quest terminology, this is tantamount to the journey to the underworld, the acknowledgment of death's grip on life. Together with this knowledge comes the understanding that one is somehow other than either death or life. This "other" is the prism's "soul." The prism's questionable compensation for his fall into self-consciousness is his realization that he has a soul. This soul is the "proof" and the "child" of his existence.

The prism can now see clearly what he is—a soul feeding off of a body. The egg about his mouth symbolizes the innocent embryo he once was, which has been devoured by experience. As the body devours its potential, so it is itself devoured in time's fire, represented here by the smoke rising between the fingers and from the nostrils of the supine body. Life feeds off of the body, as a fire feeds off of a log. The prism as body does not refract light but deflects it "through years of vacancy." These years are precisely the life-span of the impervious body, which is "all too human." The soul hates the body's animal weakness, but it needs the body in order to exist. Body and soul are "each at the other's utter mercy." Being may be a prison-house, but it is the only house one knows. The prism is devoted to the task of living, but with a broken heart.

The poet-as-prism has earned his tears through his acceptance of the necessity of being. At the conclusion of the poem, the poet reassumes his identity as a fallible and mortal being, having decided that he can live with the knowledge of his fallibility and mortality. The acceptance of necessity is this poet's skeptical rendering of the hero's return home and the completion of his quest.

"Prism" is an early version of the quest in Merrill's work. Later versions are more elaborate, culminating in the enormous trilogy, *The Changing Light at Sandover*. The basic quest pattern remains constant throughout. These poems begin with an initiating crisis and proceed through various levels of hard-earned self-knowledge to their conclusions. These conclusions are the poet's visions of "home," "paradise," or "happily ever after" in the quest pattern. Merrill's conclusions are characterized by a wry pathos. He seems not so much resigned as amenable, willing to concede that "whatever had been, had been right" (CL 63). His victory lies in choosing to abide by necessity. His version of paradise is highly qualified and hard-pressed, the paradise of an unbeliever compelled to construct something in which he can believe, if only momentarily.

2

Heroes without Name or Origin: The Quest in Merrill's Early Work

One might well say of James Merrill what Lionel Trilling noted of E. M. Forster, that "He is sometimes irritating in his refusal to be great" (4). As with Forster, Merrill's command of his medium is beyond dispute. In an early assessment, James Dickey grudgingly observed "with what fastidious, almost disdainful ease Merrill can move in whatever verse form he wishes" (99). As Dickey implied, such prodigious skill can work against a writer. When reading through Merrill's poems, we sometimes wish that he had indulged in less conspicuous cleverness, if only to assure us of his good intentions toward the less sophisticated reader. We question his motives in producing such elaborate metaphorical facades and rightly wonder what is hidden behind those walls.

Merrill knowingly and humorously acknowledges the purported limitations of his work in his introduction to *The Book of Ephraim*:

> My downfall was "word-painting." Exquisite
> Peek-a-boo plumage, limbs aflush from sheer
> Bombast unfurling through the troposhere
> Whose earthward denizens' implosion startles
> Silly quite a little crowd of mortals
> —My readers, I presumed from where I sat
> In the angelic secretariat.
> The more I struggled to be plain, the more
> Mannerism hobbled me. (CL 4)

Merrill's clever manipulation of language is inherently defensive and potentially deceptive in nature. His mannerism is a barrier to the unintelligent or single-minded reader.

By temperament, Merrill is drawn to favor intelligence over sincerity as the measure of his art. In *The (Diblos) Notebook*, he writes, "The only solution is to be very, very intelligent" (146). Merrill belongs to the party of T. S. Eliot, Henry James, and Oscar Wilde, artists who temperamentally distrusted sincerity, which is too often and easily used, according to Wilde, as an excuse for stupidity:

> We are dominated by the fanatic, whose worst vice is his sincerity. Anything approaching to the free play of the mind is practically unknown amongst us. People cry out against the sinner, yet it is not the sinful, but the stupid, who are our shame. There is no sin except stupidity. (1,057)

Merrill's clever and difficult poetry serves to cast doubt upon poetry that is emphatically sincere (one thinks of William Wordsworth and Walt Whitman in the last century and of William Carlos Williams and his heirs in this one), if at the cost of occasionally flattering the merely intelligent.

Merrill manages to save himself from charges of insincerity by turning his vast intelligence back upon itself. He is his own restless analyst. In poem after poem, the poet assumes a dual role as one who asserts and one who denies. He is both Narcissus and Echo. His insistent punning serves to emphasize the duplicity inherent in language itself, to the point at which any assertion seems to bear innately the seed of its own destruction.

In his obsession with the instability of language, Merrill again proves himself the heir of Eliot, James, and Wilde. Many of the figures in Merrill's poems seem to have originated in a Jamesian or Wildean drawing room. But the milieu in Merrill's created world is brasher than that of James and more vicious than Wilde's. Merrill's characters have grown weary of themselves and have turned cannibalistic out of boredom. Consider the poem "A Narrow Escape," from his third volume, which I quote in full:

> During a lull at dinner the vampire frankly
> Confessed herself a symbol of the inner
> Adventure. An old anxiousness took hold
> Like a mesmerist hissing for each of us
> To call up flitterings from within,
> Crags and grottos, an olive dark that lured
> Casements to loosen gleamings onto the Rhine.
> More fluently than water she controlled
> The vista. Later, von Blon said he had known

Her expressionless face before, her raven braids
—But where? A tale . . . a mezzotint? The tone
Was that of an 1830 pianoforte.
There followed for each a real danger of falling
Into the oubliette of that bland face,
Perfectly warned of how beneath it lay
The bat's penchant for sleeping all day long
Then flying off upon the wildest tangents
With little self-preserving shrieks, also
For ghastly scenes over letters and at meals,
Not to speak of positive evil, those nightly
Drainings of one's life, the blood, the laugh,
The cries for pardon, the indifferences—
And all performed with such a virtuoso's
Detachment from say their grandmother's experience
That men in clubs would snort incredulously
Provided one escaped to tell the story.
It was then Charles thought to wonder, peering over
The rests of venison, what on earth a vampire
Means by the inner adventure. Her retort
Is now a classic in our particular circle. (SP 32)

In which circle of Hell do the damned suffer ennui? This poem implicitly questions how far one will go in an attempt to escape boredom. Merrill's poetry is both the product and a critique of our overfed late-century society. Many of the poems are striving to account for, and to apologize for, their very existence.

Note the ironic confession with which the above poem begins: The central character's vampirism is taken for granted, whereas her confession to be a symbol of the inner adventure is looked upon with horror. How far we have come from Percy Shelley's spirited anointing of the poet as the true legislator of mankind. On the contrary, Merrill repeatedly charges himself (and, by implication, all poets) with arranging for "chills and fever, passions and betrayals, / Chiefly in order to make song of them" (SP 165).

Merrill's doubt as to the moral rightness of the poet's relationship to experience serves to emphasize the difficulty with which the skeptical late-century poet composes at all. Ours is the "Age of Anxiety" (CP 447), as W. H. Auden so presciently put it. This poem displays the anxiety the contemporary poet feels and the risk he takes when he assumes responsibility for addressing the "bland face" of the blank page. What after all has become of the imagination that Shelley insisted could reduce necessity to a mere vacancy, and through which Blake saw eternity in a grain of sand? Our modernist ancestors were less insistent, less certain. Wallace Stevens is representative of his generation in his equivocal response: "The mind has added nothing to human nature. It is a violence from within that protects us from a violence without. It is the imagination pressing back against the pressure of reality" (NA 36). Auden goes even further in seeking to negate the romantic legacy. We recall his famous debunking pronouncements: "Poetry makes nothing happen" (CP 248), and "The truest poetry is the most feigning" (CP 619).

Merrill has inherited Auden's skepticism but not his High Anglican moral certainty. Rather, Merrill's ambivalence, when faced with issues of right and wrong, is typically American and can be traced back through T. S. Eliot and Henry James to Nathaniel Hawthorne and our Puritan ancestors. For all his metaphorical inventiveness, Merrill harbors a deep-seated distrust of the imagination and its power over the creative artist.

To Merrill, the imagination's powers are Faustian, vampiric, rather than Promethean. The poet who avails himself of these powers is making a dangerous bargain "with positive evil." Having made his pact with the devil, he is defenseless against "those nightly / Drainings of one's life" on which the imagination feeds. The poet struggles to "escape" his skeptical temperament long enough to tell his "story," but, in the process, he is made vulnerable to escapism, "the cries for pardon, the indifferences," proffered by the power of imagination.

Merrill gives us a more subtle and explicitly autobiographical version of this Faustian bargain in "A Tenancy":

> I sat, head thrown back, and with the dried stains
> Of light on my own cheeks, proposed
> This bargain with—say with the source of light:
> That given a few years more
> (Seven or ten or, what seemed vast, fifteen)
> To spend in love, in a country not at war,
> I would give in return
> All I had. All? A little sun
> Rose in my throat. The lease was drawn.
>
> I did not feel the time expire. (SP 87)

Merrill half-heartedly conceals his pact with the devil in this passage by his coy reference to Lucifer as the source of light. Nevertheless, the nature of the bargain becomes clear as the lease is drawn. We cannot help but hear a "leash" being drawn tight around the sun/son who is the strangled heir of this agreement. The sun/son, which is rising toward inevitable eclipse, is also the poetic speech made possible by a bargain with the source of light, the power of imagination that "brings to light" what lives as potential within us.

Whatever the questionable ramifications of this bargain, the poet finds that his years of experience have already exacted their payment from him:

> The body that lived through that day
> And the sufficient love and relative peace
> Of those short years, is now not mine.
> Would it be called a soul? (SP 87)

Merrill is surely referring here to John Keats' assertion that existence in this "World of Pains and troubles" is necessary to "make" a soul (550). But Merrill cannot accept without qualification Keats' economy of necessity. For Merrill, making a soul is the same as losing it.

The fear of loss and the innate knowledge of its certainty form the skeptical foundation of Merrill's most profound poetic utterance. In an early poem, a child with "white ideas of swans" finds himself inexorably drawn to a "black swan" (SP 3). Through metaphorical ingenuity, the poet transforms the black swan from a symbol of "time's damage" into a "black plume," symbolic of "time's grief" (SP 3). For Merrill, this is the use of poetry, to make loss bearable.

No sooner is an object apprehended by this skeptical consciousness than it is declared unobtainable through the act of comprehension itself. In his poetry, Merrill traces the ways in which the mind defeats itself in this manner, while searching for a way to defeat the mind's inhibiting skepticism. The famed difficulty of Merrill's poetry is an indication of the lengths to which this poet will go in his struggle to out-distance the knowing mind. The unwieldy apparatus of the Ouija-board might be understood, in this sense, to be the ultimate effort of the poet's unconscious will to escape the death-grip of consciousness.

We can trace, through all of Merrill's work, the poet's quest to overcome his life-denying skepticism, while implicitly asserting that such skepticism is necessitated by life itself. This dual effort is at work in the lovely, brief poem "Log":

> Then when the flame forked like a sudden path
> I gasped and stumbled, and was less.
> Density pulsing upward, gauze of ash,
> Dear light along the way to nothingness,
> What could be made of you but light, and this? (SP 189)

The forking of the flame is the catastrophe that divides the self from its origins, resulting in the consciousness of loss. The realization of loss and the recognition of the self's inevitable journey to "nothingness" spurs the defensive maneuver of the poem's creation, artistic creation being one of the few acts available to the conscious self bounded by necessity.

The self's creation—in this case, its poem—is fortunately "lost in translation" (SP 278) from life to death. The poem represents the difference between the self that was and the self that is, the only conclusive evidence the poet retains that he was alive as a self yesterday, although as a different self, one that has been consumed in time's fire. As Alice says to the Gryphon: "I can tell you my adventures beginning from this morning . . . but it's no use going back to yesterday, because I was a different person then" (Carroll 97). The limitations of a poem like "Log" are acknowledged by the poet with his concluding, rhetorical question: "What could be made of you but light, and this?" He seems to apologize for the paucity of the poem's offering while implicitly accusing his skeptical temperament of turning every attempt to counter loss into a defeat.

Here, as everywhere in poetry, the enabling metaphor is the limiting metaphor. The restrictions of this poem are self-imposed, but, in their condensed form, they serve to heighten our awareness of the restrictiveness of poetic metaphor in general. Merrill's skeptical poetic consciousness fights a losing battle in which every brief, metaphorical victory serves to heighten his sense of impending and inevitable defeat. It is little wonder that he employs the vampire as his symbol for the poetic imagination. For Merrill, the poet is a lost soul whose creative victories are necessarily pyrrhic.

Given this poet's daunting temperamental opposition to the creative act, we may well wonder at his life-long devotion to it. He seems compelled by his rigorous intellectual honesty to trace his skepticism to its source, embarking upon the one quest in which defeat is inevitable. Taking the supremacy of loss as his guiding star, he naturally steers clear of the "outer" adventure, the life of the public man who is compelled along his course by the false god of the profit motive. The public man convinces himself of the "winnability" of his race; he is inherently self-deceived. This is true for all public men. Outside of the inner adventure, one's vocation is unimportant. The Wall Street broker and the nuclear activist are both guided by their respective profit motives.

Merrill employs all manner of metaphor to the same end: the furtherance of his private quest in the inner adventure. The object of this quest is the finding of what will suffice to make life imaginatively supportable. Merrill's definition of what will suffice is typically both domestic and skeptical; he calls it "the dull need to make some kind of house / Out of the life lived, out of the love spent" (SP 59). The word "spent" here alerts us to what is perhaps the central trope in Merrill's work, profit and loss, a travesty of the major Christian trope, salvation and loss. Merrill's skeptical replacement of the quest for salvation with the economics of the marketplace would again remind us of the gulf separating the contemporary poetic temperament from its romantic inheritance. Lord Byron's Manfred, the prototypic romantic figure, insists upon damning himself. Merrill's characters are damned at conception.

This poet's innate belief in the primacy and irrefutability of loss confines him to the temporal world, from which he is redeemed only in rare moments of vision. These are the moments of the sublime when the temporal and the eternal intersect, reassuring the poet that nothing is lost. But these are moments only. By contrast, a visionary poet like Blake refuses to allow the temporal even a partial dominance over the imagination and insists upon seeing eternity in every moment. If Blake were to read Merrill's epic trilogy, he would no doubt accuse the contemporary poet of a lack of faith, a self-condemning passivity in the face of necessity.

In response to the visionary's charges, Merrill might well point to the assertion of Wilde in "The Critic as Artist":

> It is enough that our fathers believed. They have exhausted the faith-faculty of the species. Their legacy to us is the skepticism of which they were afraid. Had they put it into words, it might not live within us as thought. . . . We cannot go back to the saint. There is far more to be learned from the sinner. (1,040)

The contemporary poet's journey is the journey through unbelief, and his most powerful weapon in his quest is the very skepticism that his poetic forefathers, the great visionaries, scorned.

Like Proust, Merrill is self-consciously seeking to use his art to rescue what has been lost in living. The power of translation from death to life is available to the creative artist who would painstakingly transform the waste of time into something beautiful, aspiring, and lasting:

> Those hours were not in vain
> So long as you retain
> A lightness once they're lost;
> Like one who, thinking, spends
> His inmost dividends
> To grow at any cost. (LS 74)

The poet's ability to "grow" and to transform "time's damage" in the process does come at a "cost." He must *spend* his "inmost dividends," his precious memories and loved ones, in order to preserve them in the work of art, the artist's "reliquary" (CL 77).

Merrill is ill at ease with this use of self and other that poetry requires of its practitioners. In a world in which the poet can rely on no encompassing moral vision of life to guarantee the "rightness" of the creative effort, the individual poet, concerned with the creation of an inner vision, finds himself forced to account for his creative aggression, his use of life for art. Merrill's "discovery" of the otherworldly voices could be considered an elaborate attempt by his guilty conscience to offer itself as the material for another's creative aggression, in the same manner that Henry James so often claimed to have been possessed by his subject matter.

Merrill's status as an artist with a moral passion has not been properly considered. Early critics were misled by the poet's diffident manner. Merrill's adoption of a public persona in *The Changing Light at Sandover* prompted an alarming number of critics to err in the opposite direction, reading the poem as a modern *Commedia* drawing together our multiple worlds into a universal moral vision. Despite their structural parallels, *The Changing Light* is not truly comparable to the *Commedia*. Merrill's poem is concerned primarily with the possibility of living a moral life in a world in which the very foundations of belief are necessarily relative and individual. Indeed, Merrill repeatedly undermines his own efforts to rival Dante in creating a vision of universal morality. If this poem succeeds in speaking for all of us, then it does so by insisting on the primacy of the personal viewpoint and on the inadequacy of any moral system that is not based upon the inner adventure of the private life.

If we do not read Merrill as primarily a poet of the inner adventure, then we will find ourselves unable to account for the trilogy's disturbing and politically insensitive public pronouncements, such as Mirabell's off-hand and unrefuted defense of tyranny. Alternatively, we may make the equally grave mistake of taking the spirits' user-friendly mythical system to be a less tragic, more life-affirming version of Dante's or Blake's mythos, as Jacoff seems to do when she contemplates the fact that Maria, the epic's most endearing figure, is saved at the poem's conclusion: "It is as if Dante had saved Vergil after all. Maria's fate, like Vergil's, had seemed the tragedy within the comedy, a haunting reminder of all that cannot be finally reconciled within the poem's affirmative ethos" (151). Maria's salvation stands not as an affirmation so much as a condemnation of Merrill's celestial system. A world in which all are saved is a world in which salvation is meaningless. This is the skeptic import of the poem's conclusion in which "each of the major figures is granted his wish" (Jacoff 156). Such wish-fulfillment is not to be found in Dante or Blake. Virgil is always damned; Urizen is forever coldly reasoning and self-condemned.

Jacoff further muses that "Dante's compartmentalizing imagination is alien to Merrill's propensity for turning things on their heads" (157). And yet, Dante's "compartmentalizing" enables him to separate the damned from the blessed. Merrill's anarchical hierarchy potentially damns us all, as one of the poem's more observant characters recognizes: "Is Heaven's interface / What your new friends tactfully don't call Hell?" (CL 256).

The elaborate mythical system of Merrill's poem is based upon this dependent relationship between heaven and hell. His is the poetry of love *and* loss, and it is founded on the Proustian dictum that we may only know love *by* loss. In such a world, the only true paradises are those that have been lost.

Suffering is the price the poet pays for his entrance into the lost paradises of the inner adventure. Merrill's is often the poetry of exquisite anguish. In this way, he resembles Algernorn Charles Swinburne, although his poetry is never somnambulist like Swinburne's, and is only rarely and tangentially concerned with psychological paralysis and physical decay.

These rare instances are found most often in Merrill's early work, as in the poem "Medusa," which begins: "The head, of course, had fallen to disrepair / If not to disrepute" (FFN 8). Here we see the technically precocious poet searching for his voice. Another early poem, "The Broken Bowl," begins:

> To say it once held daisies and bluebells
>   Ignores, if nothing else,
> Much diehard brilliance where, crashed to the floor,
> The wide bowl lies that seemed to cup the sun,
> Its green leaves wilted, its loyal blaze undone,
> All spilt, its glass integrity no more.
>   From piece to shattered piece
> A fledgling rainbow struggles for release.
>
> Did also the heart shatter when it slipped? (SP 6)

This is accomplished, but labored. Merrill's cast of mind is too quick for his worn subject matter addressed in such head-on fashion. His frustration with the narrow contemplative task is made evident in the opening line of the second stanza, in which he embarks upon a tedious refiguring of the first stanza's metaphor.

As with Byron and Wilde, Merrill is most acute when he is most casual, as in the later "Laboratory Poem":

> Charles used to watch Naomi, taking heart
> And a steel saw, open up turtles, live.
> While she swore they felt nothing, he would gag
> At blood, at the blind twitching, even after
> The murky dawn of entrails cleared, revealing
> Contours he knew, egg-yellows like lamps paling. (FFN 55)

The pun on "taking heart" is perhaps gratuitous, and the colloquialisms—"she swore," "he would gag"—seem forced, but there is little doubt that Merrill is on his way in this poem to finding his cautionary, clever, and equivocal voice.

We come to trust this poet more completely as his distrust of language's "misleading apparatus" grows more ingrained in his perfected use of it. Paradoxically, Merrill's poetic voice becomes more approachable as it gains authority. By the time we read the disarmingly apologetic introduction to the trilogy, "Admittedly I err by undertaking / This in its present form" (CL 3), we are beginning to feel certain that we are in the safe hands of a master.

The incorporation of error into his poetry separates Merrill's apprentice work from his mature style. In an illuminating essay, Richard Howard comments that Merrill's highly stylized early verse is "worse than vulnerable for being invulnerable" (11). Elizabeth Bishop echoes this concern in a letter to Merrill in which she generously compares his method and concerns in these early poems with that of the late James of *The Golden Bowl*, but she contends that Merrill's finely wrought bowls, "without cracks," suffer from their perfection (Bishop, L 302).

In altering his later style to allow for such imperfection, Merrill may have recalled Wilde's assertion that "it is by its very incompleteness that Art becomes complete in beauty" (1,031). Still, he also seems to have benefited from an appreciation and emulation of Bishop's work, which he has acknowledged as a poetic model, praising especially the older poet's ability to engage the reader with her "lucid, intimate tone of voice" (Merrill, Interview with Thomas Bolt 40) without becoming precious or resorting to "oracular amplification" (REC 28).

We can detect Bishop's influence in Merrill's mature voice, as in the poem "To a Butterfly," which is included in the 1962 volume, *Water Street*, the first book in which this deceptively casual voice dominates:

Already in midsummer
I miss your feet and fur.
Poor simple creature that you were,
What have you become!

Your slender person curled
About an apple twig
Rebounding to the winds' clear jig
Gave up that world

In favor of obscene
Gray matter, rode that ark
Until (as at the chance remark
Of Father Sheen)

Shining awake to slough
Your old life. And soon four
Dapper stained glass windows bore
You up—*Enough.*

Goodness, how tired one grows
Just looking through a prism:
Allegory, symbolism.
I've tried, Lord knows,

To keep from seeing double,
Blushed for whenever I did,
Prayed like a boy my cheek be hid
By manly stubble.

I caught you in a net
And first pierced your disguise
How many years ago? Time flies,
I am not yet

Proof against rigmarole.
Those frail wings, those antennae!
The day you hover without any
Tincture of soul,

Red monarch, swallowtail,
Will be the day my own
Wiles gather dust. Each will have flown
The other's jail. (SP 79–80)

There is a Mozartean sureness and easiness of manner in this clever, brief autumn elegy, but we would be mistaken to think the poem a mere trifle. As if to guard us against such a mistake, the poet's opening line contains an allusion to Dante's introduction to the *Inferno*, the butterfly's midsummer crisis paralleling Dante's mid-life confusion.

Having established the controlling analogy of butterfly to man with the title and the allusion to Dante in the first line, the poet quickly runs through the stages of the insect's transformation from caterpillar to pupa to butterfly, allowing throughout for the parallel to man's life cycle from birth to death. The caterpillar "curled / About an apple twig" would seem to represent man in his unfallen, Wordsworthian childhood, before the "obscene / Gray matter" of the rational, adult mind intervenes, blinding him to his divine origins. The transformation into the butterfly returns him heavenward, whence he came, by the symbolic means of "four / Dapper stained glass" wings.

The poet's metaphorical agility is everywhere evident in these first four stanzas. And herein lies the problem. Merrill's quickness of mind compels him to the end of his metaphor in a flight of fancy, leaving him, all too readily, face to face with the metaphor's demise—and with his own. Merrill's early poems are often little more than the ingenious working out of such an extended metaphor. These poems conclude as their metaphors die. Such a constricted method seems to foster an almost "knee-jerk" cynicism and world-weariness. Reading these poems, we cannot help but feel that the poet's conclusions—so readily arrived at—are unearned. The poet, too, seems frustrated by such constrictions.

In his mature work, Merrill more often abandons worn-out metaphors for the sake of the poem's life, as he does at the end of the fourth stanza above with his exasperated "*Enough*." This word comes at the "breaking point" of the poem when we see an inevitable metaphorical conclusion just ahead. In order to forestall such a premature and disappointing ending to his poem, the poet "turns" upon himself and begins questioning the very metaphorical method by which he has been proceeding, a method that leads him so easily to a conclusion that is a diminution of his subject and of himself.

The mature poet rebels against the metaphorical structure of his art, recognizing all too well the strictures that lie beneath this structure's "disguise" of metaphorical "rigmarole," the allegory and symbolism by which he can make time as a butterfly do his bidding. By his willingness to critique his own materials, and what he has made of them, the poet manages to abandon his metaphor before it fails *him*. His ability to leave the metaphor behind and yet continue the poem as a critique of itself may be taken as a sign of his faith in the possibilities of his craft, and by extension, of all human endeavor. The poet's faith is reflected in the poem's conclusion, which allows for hope. Death is viewed as an escape from prison for both body and soul. Such a hopeful ending would not have been possible had the poem concluded with the death of the original butterfly metaphor. This is too mechanical to allow for more than an ironic and self-defeating assertion of an afterlife (the butterfly's wings as stained glass windows rising upward).

When Merrill turns upon himself in this poem, he is performing an act that seems emblematic of his generation of poets in which an assertion is put forth and is then immediately undercut or withdrawn. This "turning upon itself" is fundamentally different from such modernist practices as Yeats' "vacillation" (Poems 249), or that typified by Stevens' dictum, "It must change" (PEM 215). Both Yeats and Stevens tend to respond to an assertion in one poem with another poem or, at the least, another stanza. But their heirs are more skeptical, barely allowing an assertion to be made before refuting it. The American poet, John Ashbery, is perhaps the most insistent of all in his use of refutation, paradox, and contradiction. The conclusion to "The Ecclesiast" is typical: "We are together at last, though far apart" (SP 60). With Merrill, this reflexive contradiction of assertion reaches a near-cacophonous level in the epic trilogy, especially in its concluding poem in which celestial hierarchies are dismantled as quickly as they are revealed.

These poets' self-refutation serves to call into doubt the ability of poetry to assert and to represent, to make a true statement about the self and the world. Elizabeth Bishop seems to have served as a model, to Merrill and Ashbery at least, of the correct skeptical attitude to assume before our late-century world. In her early poem, "Love Lies Sleeping," she sets the tone for the coming generation of poets in describing this most disturbing of visionaries: "the city grows down into his open eyes / inverted and distorted. No. I mean distorted and revealed, / if he sees it at all" (CP 17). The poem questions the very possibility of revelation in this distorted and distorting world.

Merrill seems to have learned most from Bishop's extraordinary talent for writing poems of occasion. "Poems of occasion" are not written for an occasion in public life, as are "occasional poems," but are inspired by an occasion of intense psychological and emotional import in the poet's private life. Merrill's approach toward the poem of occasion is fundamentally different from Bishop's. By examining this difference, we can determine in what way Merrill borrows from Bishop and in what way he reacts against this influence in order to claim his own creative space.

Bishop's poems of occasion are versions of the romantic poetry of correspondences; they record the rare and sublime moments in which the poetic self is able to correspond with the world at large, particularly the natural world, in which the human element seems simply one among equals with the particulars of its environment. In such a moment, the poet feels herself to be at home in the world. Too often, she feels herself to be a tourist in a world that seems the "strangest of theatres. . . . inexplicable and impenetrable, / at any view" (CP 93). Through her poetry, Bishop seeks to penetrate that landscape in order to become a part of it.

Bishop's poems often seem like lifelines thrown out in a desperate attempt to connect her interior world to the world around her. These heroic metaphorical efforts continually fail to earn the poet more than a passing acquaintance with the world at large, and the poems come to seem a record of repeated failure and small, qualified success. In the conclusion of "The Bight," the poet provides us with an illuminating metaphor of her failed attempts to connect to the world around her, as she describes the shoreline's wreckage:

> Some of the little white boats are still piled up
> against each other, or lie on their sides, stove in,
> and not yet salvaged, if they ever will be, from the last bad storm,
> like torn-open, unanswered letters.
> The bight is littered with old correspondences. (CP 60)

Like Emily Dickinson, Bishop is complaining that her letters to the world too often elicit no response. But, unlike her hermitic precursor, Bishop is willing to engage her environment on its unyielding terms, if it comes to that, rather than retreat into an interior exile.

> Click. Click. Goes the dredge,
> and brings up a dripping jawful of marl.
> All the untidy activity continues,
> awful but cheerful. (CP 60–61)

Bishop contents herself with having forced a correspondence on the "untidy" world. The poet figure does not attempt to possess the scene she witnesses, to contain the "awful but cheerful" activity of life. She satisfies herself with bearing witness to the scene, of which she herself is only a small part.

Reading such poems as "The Bight" or the haunting poem of pilgrimage "Over 2,000 Illustrations and a Complete Concordance," we might be tempted to make the overly general, if generally supportable, assertion that Bishop's nemesis is not time—what Merrill refers to in his trilogy as the poet's "nom de plume" (CL 85)—but space. She seems to accept implicitly that our knowledge of the world is necessarily time-bound, fluid, "flowing, and flown" (CP 66). But she is driven to near-despair by her limitations in *space*, by the fact that, in choosing the space in which we live "the choice is never wide and never free" (CP 94). The title of her first book, *North & South*, seems to emphasize that in choosing to live in—to correspond with—one place, we are necessarily neglecting and forsaking others.

The title of Merrill's 1966 volume, *Nights and Days*, appears to pay tribute to Bishop's, while claiming a *donnée* of its own, the world of time, as opposed to the world of space. The contrast is telling. Merrill is not attempting to correspond with the created world so much as he is striving to *possess* it, to save it from the abyss of lost time. The figure of the poet in these narratives takes on the lineaments of a heroic quester bent on saving the world from all-but-certain loss. Within his poem, the poet creates a world in which the past can live, and in which *he* can live within his past.

The occasion that provides Merrill material for these poems is most often an occasion of involuntary Proustian memory, as opposed to Bishop's occasions of Wordsworthian correspondence. In "A Tenancy," the concluding poem of *Water Street*, the poet draws the book to a close with a fitting backward glance, prompted by a vague, involuntary memory that the poem works to resurrect: "Something in the light of this March afternoon / Recalls that first and dazzling one" (SP 86). The poet's life is the subject here, and the implied method of this poem is "re-call"—memory.

By the poem's conclusion, the vaguely recalled memory has been salvaged and restored. The memory has been placed within the context of the present. By doing so, the poet assures himself of the continuity of his journey. His consolation for his many losses to time is the crucial reassurance that in his beginning is his end, which is itself a new beginning. But the present is imbued with the past at its own peril. From this poet's skeptical viewpoint, art seems to grow at life's expense. The poet of "A Tenancy" admits that he has no other choice but to use art, and to be used by it, if he is to save what is salvageable from the waste of years, if he is to satisfy his "dull need" to place his present within a larger context. The alternative is a life of abject slavery to necessity, the unimaginative god of the present devoid of its past. By *choosing* to abide by necessity, the poet is paradoxically allowed to escape necessity for the briefest moment, the moment occupied by the poem within time. In the choice itself, the poet finds his freedom: "If I am host at last / It is of little more than my own past. / May others be at home in it" (SP 88).

As Bishop's nemesis is the unyielding "space" between her interior world and the world without, so Merrill's nemesis is the movement of time, which "stops at nothing" (CL 71). The poet uses time as material, taking the memories thrown up by time's interminable flowing and making a house of them, only to have it washed away in time's flood: "Hold still, Breathes the canal. But then *it* stirs" (CL 75). In his effort to save time, the poet is fighting a losing battle, just as Bishop's effort to create a lasting correspondence with the outer world is inevitably a failure. The only possible success for either poet comes from the devotion to the struggle. By the same token, failure is the refusal to contend, prompted by a lack of faith in the goodness or rightness of the effort.

For Bishop, failure to seek a correspondence with the outer world results in homelessness, the acceptance of spiritual exile, and the role of the eternal tourist. For Merrill, the refusal to devote oneself to the struggle against time results in childlessness, a symbolic state of disconnectedness and desolation. At the conclusion of the poem "Childlessness," we are presented with a scene evoking Richard Wagner's *Götterdämmerung*, the inevitable ending to any world that denies the possibility of progeny:

> A sky stained red, a world
> Clad only in rags, threadbare,
> Dabbling the highway's ice with blood,
> A world. The cloak thrown down for it to wear
> In token of past servitude
> Has fallen onto the shoulders of my parents
> Whom it is eating to the bone. (SP 72)

The heir without progeny has refused to accept the implicit ancestral directive to carry on the line. He has denied his own heredity by forcing it back upon itself, compelling his parents to wear, like a shirt of Nessus, their consuming failure to win a vicarious immortality through reproduction.

In an otherwise equitable and elucidating essay, Harold Bloom contends that guilt and grief are not "Merrillean" emotions (Introduction 2). This passage from "Childlessness" would certainly seem to belie such a reading of the poet's work. Merrill's poetry repeatedly expresses both grief and guilt, but in a resigned, humorous, and self-knowing manner that seems intended to deflect attention from the disturbing emotions at its origin. Merrill's elaborate efforts to disguise the emotional "catastrophes" that we feel reside at the heart of so much of his work seem to indicate an obsession with and distrust of "origins," the ultimate example of which is the equivocal gift of heredity itself.

The poet's temperamental distrust of heredity and the inherited past leads (at least metaphorically) to his childlessness, his skeptical denial of posterity. But his refusal to propagate paradoxically and tragically ties him to his past. He has refused the one action that would allow him to resolve his Oedipal struggle with the paternal past by passing this struggle on to another generation. To placate heredity and posterity, he allows *himself* to be consumed in the sacrificial Oedipal fire. He fuels his own creation: "Art— / The tale that all but shapes itself—survives / By feeding on its personages' lives" (CL 218). By making poetry out of his Oedipal struggle, the poet is able to make destiny his choice and turn life's consuming flame into a "consuming myth" (SP 131).

In two early poems, Merrill clearly figures his temperamental opposition to biological heredity and his effort to overcome this temperamental skepticism. In the poems "Scenes from Childhood" and "The Broken Home," the poet engages his family history to tell the Oedipal tale. In "Scenes from Childhood," the poet returns us to the tale's beginning, describing a scene in which he and his mother view home-movies made thirty years before:

> We had then, a late sun,
> A door from which the primal
> Figures jerky and blurred
> As lightning bugs
> From lanterns issue, next
> To be taken for stars,
> For fates. With knowing smiles
> And beaded shrugs
>
> My mother and two aunts
> Loom on the screen. Their
> Brows pucker, their arms encircle
> One another,
> Their ashen lips move. (SP 66–67)

The sun/son of this passage is indeed "late," the latest and last. His destiny is tied to the archetypal mother figure, who is presented here along with her two sisters. Appearing as the Fates, the three sisters "loom" on the screen with "knowing smiles" and "beaded" shrugs. No hero is ever free of their encircling arms, which already have drawn the poet's father to their bosom.

> From the love seat's gloom
> A quiet chuckle escapes
> My white-haired mother

To see in that final light
A man's shadow mount
Her dress. And now she is
Advancing, sister-
less, but followed by
A fair child, or fury—
Myself at four, in tears.
I raise my fist,

Strike, she kneels down. The man's
Shadow afflicts us both.
Her voice behind me says
It might go slower.
I work dials, the film jams.
Our headstrong old projector
Glares at the scene which promptly
Catches fire.

Puzzled, we watch ourselves
Turn red and black, gone up
In a puff of smoke now coiling
Down fierce beams.
I switch them off. A silence.
Your father, she remarks,
Took those pictures; later
Says pleasant dreams,

Rises and goes. (SP 67–68)

The earth-mother has earned the right to chuckle at her timeless struggle with the sky-father figure, who represents time. She has found an ally in her mother-dominated son. As a "fury," the son is committed to seeking vengeance against his father for the "crime" against his mother. The father has forced time upon timelessness, producing the fury, his son. At his mother's behest, this son has determined to fight time in order to make it "go slower." The son's rebellion results in the defeat of time but at the cost of his own future. He is the "son and heir" of that which he has destroyed. He has brought on *Götterdämmerung*: The world "catches fire" and goes up "in a puff of smoke" because of his refusal to accept his inheritance and to pass it on to the next generation.

The mother's "pleasant dreams" as she departs for bed after having watched with her son the symbolic destruction of his future is cruelly ironic. He is left alone with his crime. Gradually, he is given to understand the full import of his patricide:

The son and heir! In the dark
It makes me catch my breath

And hear, from upstairs, hers—
That faintest hiss
And slither, as of life
Escaping into space,
Having led its characters
To the abyss

Of night. Immensely still
The heavens glisten. One broad
Path of vague stars is floating
Off, a shed skin
Of all whose fine cold eyes
First told us, locked in ours:
You are the heroes without name
Or origin. (SP 69)

By the concluding stanza, the poet-quester has come to understand that his rebellion against time has robbed him not only of his future but also of his past. He is stranded, "without name or origin," within the abyss of the present. The true nature of his archetypal mother becomes clear to him. She is the snake in the grass whose "hiss and slither" have led him to this abyss. She represents his unwilled fate and unwitting "fall."

In "The Broken Home," the poet tells the story of his struggle to resurrect his lost name and origin. Since he has been bred to error, his only hope for salvation resides in the possibility of *willing* his fall. In the first of the poem's seven sonnets, the poet depicts the "break" in consciousness, or "fall" into the unconscious, that marks the first stage of his quest:

Crossing the street,
I saw the parents and the child
At their window, gleaming like fruit
with evening's mild gold leaf.

In a room on the floor below,
Sunless, cooler—a brimming
Saucer of wax, marbly and dim—
I have lit what's left of my life.

I have thrown out yesterday's milk
And opened a book of maxims.
The flame quickens. The word stirs.

Tell me, tongue of fire,
That you and I are as real
At least as the people upstairs. (SP 109)

The family in the window "gleaming like fruit" prompts the poet's identity crisis by reminding him of his own "fruitlessness." A child provides its parents with irrefutable proof of the self's substantiality. According to Freud, "At the most touchy point in the narcissistic system, the immortality of the ego, which is so hard pressed by reality, security is achieved by taking refuge in the child" (FR 556). William Shakespeare too repeatedly returned to this point in the sonnets when addressing the childless fair youth: "For having traffic with thyself alone, / Thou of thyself thy sweet self does deceive" (#4), and "Thou single wilt prove none" (#8). The poet of "The Broken Home" lacks the narcissistic reassurance of the child since he has chosen, or has been fated, to occupy a sunless/sonless room. He has no living proof of his past, nothing to show for yesterday's "milk," which we might read here as semen. But the phrase "thrown out yesterday's milk" also implies the poet's willingness to break with this past. Paradoxically, this break is made possible only by "digging up the past," as the poet begins his journey into the unconscious world of time lost.

Merrill's guide into this underworld—the "floor below" the life of the conscious present—is a "book of maxims." This indicates to us that he is making a verbal and metaphorical quest. The purpose of his quest is finally and simply to use art to save life, to rely upon the power of the quickening imaginative flame and the stirring word to make his ideal world—the world of the life that is lived in art—"as real / At least as the people upstairs," the world of the actual child he will never have, the posterity that has been sacrificed to the "tongue of fire" in order to give that flame a voice.

Upstairs is where the primal family lives, the "ideal" family that has been incorporated into the poet's ego as an ideal by which it measures itself. According to Freud, each of us is drawn to "set up an *ideal* in himself by which he measures his actual ego"; "from the point of view of the ego this formulation would be the condition of repression" (GPT 74). Freud has further asserted that the ego can successfully fight this repression, which represents societal as well as parental expectations, by accepting the essential "truth" of the ego-ideal's accusations while at the same time forcing the ego-ideal to see its hypocrisy. By such a sublimation, the ego in effect says to the ego ideal: "You are correct in your criticism of me (in Merrill's case, the ego-ideal's criticism of his childlessness) but fail to acknowledge that, since you are my own creation, and I am, in a sense, *your* creation, you, too, are culpable." Through this process of identification, the ego brings the ego-ideal back into line with its perceived reality.

Before this reidentification can occur, however, the ego-quester must come to recognize the way in which the parental figures of authority and repression, which prompted the formation of the ego-ideal, survive in the idealized psyche. In the second and third sonnets of "The Broken Home," the poet's quest is to rediscover who his parents really were and are. (The poet's actual parents and the parents who have survived in his ego-ideal are not identical, but they are necessarily related.) Merrill begins his search by seeking to define and understand his father, the primary mover, according to Freud, behind an individual's creation of the repressive ego-ideal (EI 26). We will note that the poet's quest is simultaneously into the past and into the unconscious:

> My father, who had flown in World War I,
> Might have continued to invest his life
> In cloud banks well above Wall Street and wife,
> But the race was run below, and the point was to win.
>
> Too late now, I make out in his blue gaze
> (Through the smoked glass of being thirty-six)
> The soul eclipsed by twin black pupils, sex
> And business; time was money in those days.
>
> Each thirteenth year he married, when he died
> There were already several chilled wives
> In sable orbit—rings, cars, permanent waves.
> We'd felt him warming up for a green bride.
>
> He could afford it. He was in his "prime"
> At three score ten. But money was not time. (SP 109)

The most telling phrase in this bitterly humorous sonnet is "too late now." The poet recognizes that he has inherited his father's faults. We can read the sonnet as a series of warnings to the self. The casually irreverent tone that the poet adopts toward his father serves to emphasize the son's guilty repudiation of the father's failures.

The father's world view is linear. He thinks of life as a race with and against time, which is given tangible form in the world "below" as "money." The point of the race is "to win" as much money as possible in the time provided. The father's abrupt death at the end of the sonnet alerts us to the danger of living life according to this linear model: for money is not time.

The archetypal sky-father is by nature ignorant of death. Northrop Frye has written that the sky-father lives in "a world made, not born" (SS 112). To him, the sun rises miraculously each morning and disappears, just as miraculously, each night. By contrast, the earth-mother's world is dependent on the morning-to-night, birth-to-death cycle for continuation. From her point of view, death is not only natural, but necessary. The poet's father aligns himself with this archetypal feminine cycle by virtue of his marriage to a "green bride" every thirteen years, resulting in his several "chilled wives / In sable orbit." But the main thrust of his life is linear, and we find an inherent and tragic irony in the fact that, despite his best efforts to outgrow the "cloud banks" of his origins, he must make the cyclical return through his death to the eternal world he has forsaken. The father's ultimate failure is the result of his near-total investment in the time-bound race below, which causes him to lose sight of his divine and immortal origins.

The father turns a blind eye to the eternal. His "soul" has been "eclipsed by twin black pupils, sex / And business." In the terms of the Freudian family drama upon which Merrill is so obviously drawing for this poem, the father's business *is* sex. His blindness represents the Oedipal struggle that he has inherited and is seeking to pass on to his children. But he encounters opposition in his poet-son. The son's early observation of his father's blindness has prompted his own decision to remain childless. Seeing how his father was deceived by the self-created mirror of sex and business—the image given is of one staring into a mirror in which the pupil of the eye sees only the endless "black hole" of itself reflected back—the child chooses to avoid creating a self-deceiving mirror of his own.

But the psychological self requires narcissistic reflection in order to believe in its very existence. In this poem, we see how the poet is attempting to create, in and through art, a substitute mirror for the child-mirror he has forsaken. The poet's effort to create such a mirror proves that he is no longer simply rebelling against heredity. He has decided to accept his inheritance, if only in the poem, which becomes the symbol of the missing child and the poet's payment to posterity.

Such a view of the creative act is essentially anti-Freudian. Freud would have us view any artistic effort as a defensive maneuver in the face of heredity, the ubiquitous father. Merrill seems to be following his earlier and more primary influence, Oscar Wilde, in adopting a more enabling view of heredity in this poem. In *The Critic as Artist,* Wilde argued that the artist creates his "mirror" not as a reaction *against* heredity but as an action *enabled by* heredity. Accepting our inherited limitations, we paradoxically earn the right to exercise free will, but only through the imagination, in the world of art and of the mind:

> Heredity has become, as it were, the warrant for the contemplative life. It has shown us that we are never less free than when we try to act. It has hemmed us round with the nets of the hunter, and written upon the wall the prophecy of our doom. We may not watch it, for it is within us. We may not see it, save in a mirror that mirrors the soul. (1,040)

The contemplative life does not guard against but simply mirrors the actions of heredity. Passive contemplation liberates through the imaginative activity it prompts. It enables us to construct a mirror within the world of the mind:

> While in the sphere of practical and external life [Heredity] has robbed energy of its freedom and activity of its choice, in the subjective sphere, where the soul is at work, it comes to us, this terrible shadow, with many gifts, gifts of strange temperaments and subtle susceptibilities, gifts of wild ardours and chill moods of indifference, complex multiform gifts of thought that are at variance with each other, and passions that war against themselves. (1,040)

The ambivalence inherent in all true art, its "wild ardours and chill moods," is at least the partial result of "this terrible shadow," heredity, which cannot be conquered but may be appeased. The imaginative effort of appeasement guarantees our freedom within what Wallace Stevens called the "vital boundary, in the mind" (PEM 368).

Merrill continues his work of appeasement within "The Broken Home" by distancing himself from his parents, allowing them to stand apart as universal archetypes. This maneuver in the third sonnet enables the poet to envision his parents as victims of necessity, like himself.

> When my parents were younger this was a popular act:
> A veiled woman would leap from an electric, wine-dark car
> To the steps of no matter what—the Senate or the Ritz Bar
> And bodily, at newsreel speed, attack
>
> No matter whom—Al Smith or Jose Maria Sert
> Or Clemenceau—veins standing out on her throat
> As she yelled *War monger! Pig! Give us the vote!*,
> And would have to be hauled away in her hobble skirt.
>
> What had the man done? Oh, made history.
> Her business (he had implied) was giving birth,
> Tending the house, mending the socks.
>
> Always the same old story—
> Father Time and Mother Earth,
> A marriage on the rocks. (SP 110)

The poet gives us a general and archetypal view of the struggle between the sexes. The woman is veiled, faceless, and her story is the same the world round, as the poet makes clear with the three male names, each of a different ethnic origin. She emerges from a "wine-dark car," an allusion to Homer's wine-dark sea, the mother of us all and the mythological origin of Venus, the goddess of love, who is mythically responsible for the struggle between man and woman. This ongoing struggle is suggested by the "electric" quality of the car. An electric current requires opposing poles, positive and negative, male and female. The man's crime is making "history," conducting the business of society and culture, while the woman is "tending the house," protecting her natural and archetypal interests.

The child's role in this primal struggle becomes clear in sonnet four, in which the poet recreates the child's Oedipal drama:

> One afternoon, red, satyr-thighed
> Michael, the Irish setter, head
> Passionately lowered, led
> The child I was to a shut door.
>
> Blinds beat sun from the bed.
> The green-gold room throbbed like a bruise.
> Under a sheet, clad in taboos
> Lay whom we sought, her hair undone, outspread,
>
> And of a blackness found, if ever now, in old
> Engravings where the acid bit.
> I must have needed to touch it
> Or the whiteness—was she dead?
> Her eyes flew open, startled strange and cold.
> The dog slumped to the floor. She reached for me. I fled. (SP 110)

We have returned from the world of mythical archetype to the private world of Merrill's childhood. Merrill tells us elsewhere, perhaps facetiously, that the scene described in this sonnet is based upon memories of a childhood poem: "I had written at least one poem when I was seven or eight. It was a poem about going with the Irish setter into my mother's room—an episode that ended up in 'The Broken Home'" (REC 74). Whether the products of fact or fiction, the sonnet's figures are symbolic of the *archetypal* struggle between mother and son. Michael, the Irish setter, represents the child's "animal" instincts in the poem. He is "satyr-thighed" with head "passionately lowered," and he leads the child on an instinctive "hunt" that brings them to the mother's door. Once inside this shut door, the child finds a room full of Oedipal symbols. The blinds that "beat the sun" from the bed remind us that this son faces Oedipal "blindness" if he succumbs to his instincts and allows the mother to exert control over him. She wants to pit him against his father in an unwinnable battle for dominion. Failure to oppose the mother at this critical stage leads to psychological handicap, symbolized by Oedipus' blindness.

The child in this sonnet symbolically defeats his mother by escaping from her grasp. He undergoes a crisis of individuation in which he forces a separation between himself and his mother. In cultural terms, the son must be willing to forego maternal care in order to break with the family and become a member of society. From a psychological perspective, the son must remove himself from his position as an object for the mother's unconscious projections. He must force her to contend with him on equal terms as an individual psyche. In the terms of the quest-romance, the son must learn to love, not simply be loved.

In this drama of individuation, the archetypal mother figure is the necessary antagonist. In mythical terms she is the Great Mother, the vengeful Aphrodite in the tale of Psyche and Eros. Psychologically, she represents the unconscious, both individual and collective, against which the ego strives. Jung's label for the Great Mother figure is the "destructive anima." In *The Book of Ephraim*, several figures display her characteristics (CL 35).

The mother in "The Broken Home" is given identifying attributes of this destructive mother archetype. Her hair is unnaturally dark, "of a blackness found, if ever now, in old / Engravings where the acid bit." The "acid" and the "blackness" here symbolically align the mother with the potentially destructive and consuming libidinal drives of the unconscious. When the mother wakes up, her eyes are significantly "startled strange and cold," causing the dog to slump to the floor. The dog's reaction represents the child's suppressed sexual instinct. The child's recognition of the danger inherent in the mother's consuming love and his subsequent flight signal the beginning of his quest for a personalized Eros. He seeks a love based on choice, not necessity.

In the second, third, and fourth sonnets in the sequence, the poet-quester attempts to reacquaint himself with the archetypal parental figures in his psyche. He engages in a dual process of willfully distancing himself from these figures while consciously reidentifying with them and admitting their continuing influence in the mature self. His quest is fraught with dangers. The danger he faces in his encounter with the father is his tendency to dismiss and ridicule him, whereas the mother threatens to overcome the quester with her overpowering possessiveness. Despite the inherent dangers of the task, the quester has succeeded by the conclusion of the first four sonnets in identifying with the father's failures and refusing the mother's consuming love. He is poised for the final stage of his journey, the birth of a new self born of choice and not of necessity.

At the beginning of the fifth sonnet, we find the poet figured as a child in an upstairs bedroom, looking down from a window at his parents on the driveway below. The situation presented in the first sonnet, in which the poet on the street looks up at the family in the window, prompting his crisis, is reversed, suggesting the poet's newly won conquest over heredity.

> Tonight they have stepped out onto the gravel.
> The party is over. It's the fall
> Of 1931. They love each other still.
>
> She: Charlie, I can't stand the pace.
> He: Come on, honey—why, you'll bury us all.
>
> A lead soldier guards my windowsill:
> Khaki rifle, uniform and face.
> Something in me grows heavy, silvery, pliable.
>
> How intensely people used to feel!
> Like metal poured at the close of a proletarian novel,
> Refined and glowing from the crucible,
> I see those two hearts, I'm afraid,
> Still. Cool here in the graveyard of good and evil,
> They are even so to be honored and obeyed. (SP 111)

In the first line of the sonnet, the poet positions his parents together "on the rocks" of marital strife and archetypal opposition. In the second line he employs the colloquial "The party is over" and the mythical "It's the fall" to alert us to the crucial nature of what is about to occur.

Merrill's parents divorced while he was still a child, but this sonnet is only superficially concerned with the parents' drama. The primary issue here is the parents' effect on the child, who feels torn between them. In Jung's system the archetypal male parent represents the ego, while the female represents the unconscious, both of whom seek dominance in the self. In the poet's refiguring of his family drama, he makes these opposed figures "love each other still." By doing so, the poet figures his return to a prelapsarian psychic state, before the development of consciousness, at which point the unconscious and conscious selves become estranged. He is placing himself in position to "fall" again so that he may do so consciously and willingly, turning what was necessity into an act of volition.

The poet overhears his parents' conversation. The accusations made by each against the other are the same accusations the ego and unconscious have continually leveled at one another. The feminine unconscious complains that she "can't stand the pace"; she resents being used in the masculine ego's linear, time-bound race for worldly success and sexual conquest. The masculine ego in turn speaks the unsavory truth when he claims that his wife, who stands here for both the psychic unconscious and the mythic Earth Mother, will "bury us all." The poet-quester hears both sides of the argument and understands that both figures, father and mother, ego and unconscious, are constrained by their natures. He recognizes that the collision between linear and cyclical world views, one based on reason and the other on instinct, is unavoidable. Understanding that no one is to blame for the psychic trauma caused by the archetypal opposition of the ego and unconscious, the poet is able to forgive both father and mother at once. This amounts to the forgiveness and acceptance of the dual nature within himself.

Merrill employs alchemical imagery to figure the poet's transformation into a psychically mature adult who accepts responsibility for both his gift from heredity and his debt to posterity. The lead soldier that "guards" the windowsill represents not only the poet's defensiveness in regard to his ancestry but also the "base" material that is imaginatively internalized and transformed into "something" inside the poet that "grows heavy, silvery, pliable." A basic knowledge of the alchemical process leads us to the secret of this transformation. We recognize that the "heavy, silvery, pliable" material is quicksilver or Mercury, the god of alchemical transformation. According to Jung, who seems to have influenced Merrill in his use of alchemical symbolism here and elsewhere, Mercury represents "the process by which the lower and material is transformed into the higher and spiritual" (AS 237). He refers to this spirit as the symbol of the collective unconscious and as the mythical source of both good and evil, salvation and damnation (AS 247). For our purposes in reading this poem, we may justifiably consider Mercury to be the mythical symbol of Wilde's "heredity," the double-edged gift of human nature.

With the appearance of Mercury in sonnet five, the poet is given to understand the full weight of his inheritance and exclaims, "How intensely people used to feel!" With this statement, he alerts us to a fresh danger in his quest to choose necessity—the lure of the mythical Golden Age. Frye has called such idealized mythologizing of the past "projected Romance" and argued that a quester who succumbs to its allure will believe the past to be "the mirror of the future" (SS 177). Such a belief leads to the idealization of heredity and posterity and to the denigration of the present. The quester who would choose necessity must exalt the present as the freely willed life of the mind, separable from heredity, a mirror that reflects reality only.

The poet recognizes this separation at the end of sonnet five when he asserts that we live our private lives, the life of the mind, in the "graveyard of good and evil." By saying so, he implicitly accepts that being is necessarily greater than its categories. The poet nonetheless recognizes that these categories may not be successfully evaded. He may not *be* his parents, but "They are even so to be honored and obeyed."

> . . . Obeyed, at least, inversely. Thus
> I rarely buy a newspaper, or vote.
> To do so, I have learned, is to invite
> The tread of a stone guest within my house.
>
> Shooting this rusted bolt, though, against him,
> I trust I am no less time's child than some
> Who on the heath impersonate Poor Tom
> Or on the barricades risk life and limb.
>
> Nor do I try to keep a garden, only
> An avocado in a glass of water—
> Roots pallid, gemmed with air. And later,
>
> When the small gilt leaves have grown
> Fleshly and green, I let them die, yes, yes,
> And start another. I am earth's no less. (SP 111)

In this sonnet the poet-quester attempts to defend his childlessness, the poem's originating crisis, after having reestablished relations with the parental authorities who live on in the idealized psyche. He begins by silently addressing the archetypal father-figure, whose overwhelming influence, "the tread of a stone guest," can only be escaped by attempted negation. Like Don Giovanni, the poet-quester becomes a martyr in the service of delinquency. By *not* buying a newspaper and *not* voting, the son implicitly questions the roles that his father confidently assumed.

Becoming a sinful skeptic is one of the least destructive ways to escape the father's overwhelming influence. One can act out one's rebellion "on the barricades," attacking the father figure directly, but at the risk of "life and limb." Alternatively, one may direct the aggression inward and become "mad" like Poor Tom, but madness leads to self-destruction. Faced with such alternatives, the poet has chosen the skepticism of the sinner. In an age of unbelief, such skepticism becomes a paradoxical act of faith. The creative artist's solipsistic rebellion against family and society is offered as evidence of his devotion to culture and history, proving that he is indeed "time's child."

Having made his symbolic peace with Father Time, the poet-quester has still to appease Mother Earth. Her realm of the individual and collective unconscious is immune to the anxieties of time but is rife with the dangers of the conflicting libidinal drives. According to Freud, the potentialities for life and death, procreation and destruction, reside side by side in the unconscious. The psychically healthy individual must continually balance one against the other. The procreative urge for this poet remains potential. Nevertheless, he can placate the urge through his imaginative creations in poetry. He may also placate the death-urge imaginatively, as each created poem is abandoned. The "avocado" is prompted to sprout leaves and then left to die. Small wonder that the leaves are described as "gilt." The poet ruthlessly abandons his creations when they begin to take on a "life of their own." His is the guilt of the parent who must, in fairness, accept a child's anger, since the child did not choose to be born but was the product of the parent's narcissistic demand for projection (if not of blind desire).

Having realized his responsibility and culpability as a "parent" of imaginative works, the poet finds himself able to reidentify with the family "at their window," from whom he was estranged at the poem's inception. Understanding that his parents' guilt is his own, he can view himself as a psychic "whole," as parent and child at once, both guilty and innocent. The acceptance of this paradox indicates a willingness to acknowledge the inherent contrariness of the self, which is essentially dual: conscious and unconscious, masculine and feminine. The poet makes the dual identification explicit in the sonnet's concluding line: "I am earth's no less." No less? No less than he is "time's," and no less than anyone else who has been given the unsought gift of life.

In these first six sonnets, the poet recounts his journey to and return from the underworld. Having withstood the trials of psychic dissolution in order to choose to be reborn, he is now in a position to conclude his "story" and to tell it abroad, as he is fated to do, like the ancient mariner. Throughout the poem, Merrill has been at pains to balance the individual and the archetypal. With the final sonnet, he brings both stories to a single conclusion in an effort to teach what he has learned:

> A child, a red dog roam the corridors,
> Still, of the broken home. No sound. The brilliant
> Rag runners halt before wide-open doors.
> My old room! Its wallpaper—cream, medallioned

With pink and brown—brings back the first nightmares,
Long summer colds, and Emma, sepia-faced,
Perspiring over broth carried upstairs
Aswim with golden fats I could not taste.

The real home became a boarding school.
Under the ballroom ceiling's allegory
Someone at last may actually be allowed
To learn something; or, from my window, cool
With the unstiflement of the entire story,
Watch a red setter stretch and sink in cloud. (SP 112)

We all issue from "broken homes" and carry within us the warring factions: father and mother, ego and unconscious, society and family. None may escape heredity. But by an extreme effort, it is possible to make peace with heredity and actually "learn something" from the "ballroom ceiling's allegory," as Merrill asserted in an interview, in which he recalled "the story of how Cronus cuts off the scrotum, or 'ballroom,' of his father Uranus and throws it into the sea, where it begins to foam and shine, and the goddess of Love and Beauty is born" (REC 75). Before the quester can recognize, experience, or create "love and beauty," he must mature psychically by making destiny his choice. In order to do this, the poet of "The Broken Home" willingly "brings back the first nightmares," the submerged primal memories of patricide and incest that Freud insisted lie at the base of our psychic ladders. In sonnet two, the poet-quester mocks and belittles the father figure, resulting in the father's symbolic emasculation. And in sonnet four, he symbolically weds his mother by forcing open her shut door to reveal the figure "clad in taboos" that he "needed to touch."

Having earned his status as a psychically mature adult, the poet-quester can see the broken home for what it really is—a boarding school that is meant to be outgrown and left behind but not forgotten or destroyed. Accepting his inheritance, he has learned the secret to reading the ballroom ceiling's allegory, which comes from experience alone. He has, in effect, become the "head-master" at his own boarding school whose single pupil is his art, which he endows with the "entire story" of his inheritance. This is the story of the broken home itself, which becomes—through the poem—the poet's posterity. Left untold, this unborn child or poem had stifled the childless poet and prevented him from leaving childhood. But with the "unstiflement" of the story through the poem's birth, the poet has proven his devotion to heredity and posterity, to Father Time and Mother Earth. The poem's concluding image depicts the wedding of the poet's archetypal parents, of time (or memory) and eternity, as the poet's boyhood pet transforms into the sinking sun. This returns us to the poem's beginning in which the "son" "sinks" into the world of the unconscious as he crosses the street.

Harold Bloom has written in "The Internalization of Quest-Romance":

> I think that what Blake and Wordsworth do for their readers, or can do, is closely related to what Freud does or can do for his, which is to provide both a map of the mind and a profound faith that the map can be put to a saving use. (3)

In this chapter, I have attempted to trace the development of Merrill's "map of the mind," which, before *The Changing Light at Sandover*, was most intricately presented in longer poems such as "The Broken Home." Other poems of similar length, such as "The Thousand and Second Night" and "From the Cupola," are arguably finer achievements, but neither is as crucial to the poet's ongoing struggle to wrest art from life. In "The Broken Home," Merrill gives us the most straightforward version of his intensely personal poetic effort to overcome childlessness, to create a world, in and through art, that is not forever on the brink of dissolution.

This poem perhaps suffers from the poet's over-willingness to equate his actual parents with the archetypal Father Time and Mother Earth, as well as from his close adherence to the Freudian family drama. But the very familiarity of these figures allows us to see Merrill's symbolism at work translating life into art. By tracing the poet's use of material from psychology, mythology, and alchemy, we have prepared ourselves for the poet's manipulation of a much more intricate and elliptical symbolism in *The Book of Ephraim*.

In that poem, the poet's "profound faith" that the map of the mind he is creating can be put to a "saving use" is made evident by his own reliance on and devotion to the spirit Ephraim. Ephraim brings to the poet at the Ouija board a "private mythology" that makes the symbolic systems pieced together in earlier poems like "The Broken Home" seem quaint and obvious by comparison. The poet's faith in this mythology allows him to enter the borderland between life and art and to make a poetic house in that world in which the "parallels / Meet and nothing lasts and nothing ends" (SP 233).

3

The Incarnation and Withdrawal of a God: *The Book of Ephraim*

> These forms are not abortive figures, rocks,
> Impenetrable symbols, motionless. They move
>
> About the night. They live without our light
> In an element not the heaviness of time,
> In which reality is prodigy.
>
> —Wallace Stevens

Reading James Merrill's *The Changing Light at Sandover,* we find an essential difference between the first book of the trilogy, *The Book of Ephraim,* and the second and third books, *Mirabell's Books of Number* and *Scripts for the Pageant.* Merrill writes in *Mirabell* that *Ephraim* was twenty years in the making (CL 261). By contrast, in the last two volumes, he says his "nose is very close to the page. I can only hope that what I lost in 'aesthetic distance' I gained in 'immediacy.' In any case, they were too compelling for me to wait till I was seventy to write them" (REC 58). Certainly the contrast between distance and immediacy helps explain the difference that we *feel* exists between *Ephraim* and its successors. But the difference between the poems is more than can be accounted for by what the poet refers to as the "winnowing" of "time itself" in the creation of *Ephraim* (REC 64). This poem seems to have been written in a different mode altogether from *Mirabell* or *Scripts.* It is as though Merrill's conception of poetry itself changed between the writing of *The Book of Ephraim* and the earlier books of lyric poems, and the second and third books of the trilogy.

I suggest that we consider Merrill's epic trilogy as a diptych, which moves, as he himself suggests, from "Romance to Ritual" (CL 319). *The Book of Ephraim* is a Jungian quest-romance for psychic individuation, which follows the pattern set by earlier lyrics such as "Prism" and "The Broken Home." In Merrill's version of the quest-romance, the poet is seeking the romantic poet's analog of Jung's vision of psychic "wholeness," which is the romantic sublime, the moment of intersection between our mutable world and the divine. As with the quest for psychic wholeness, the quest for the sublime is always a failure when pursued at length. For even if found, the sublime is necessarily lost again in this time-bound world. The repetitions of this quest eventually lead the poet-quester of *Ephraim* to a vision in which all of life appears an endless repetition, centered upon failure.

The second and third books of the trilogy may be thought of as the poet's efforts to erase this absurdist vision of life as a clockwork existence in which free will plays no role, and to replace it with a ritualized vision of the world as ordered toward a final end that is a final good. This effort is modeled on Dante's *Divine Comedy*, but Merrill fails (as he acknowledges) where Dante succeeds. The poet's failure returns him to the quest-romance world of *Ephraim* in which the sublime moment is sought after, won, and lost. *The Book of Ephraim*, therefore, must be considered the central and crucial book in this trilogy.

The hero of *The Book of Ephraim* is the poet himself, and the "damsel in distress" is his poem. The poet as character in his own poem—to whom Merrill refers as "JM"—is only the potential author of this work. It is his quest to become the poet of this poem. The poem's completion is the climax and conclusion of this quest, at which point the character, JM, metamorphoses into the poet of *Ephraim*. The crises that must be undergone before the quest is finished include anything that would hinder the poem's composition. The final and most daunting obstacle that JM must overcome is his own unwillingness to *be* the poet of *The Book of Ephraim*.

The poet's reluctance to write *The Book of Ephraim* is visible throughout the finished poem, which begins, tellingly, "Admittedly I err by undertaking / This in its present form. The baldest prose / Reportage was called for" (CL 3). Merrill had attempted to use his experience with Ephraim (the spirit he contacts through the Ouija board) as the basis for a fictional novel instead of this autobiographical poem. But, as he writes:

> Blind
> Promptings put at last the whole mistaken
> Enterprise to sleep
> . . . .
> and I alone was left
> To tell my story. (CL 4)

When Merrill abandons his fiction in favor of autobiography, he follows the examples of Dante and Proust by refusing to allow fictional characters to inhabit his imaginative world. In *Ephraim*, he seeks to redeem his life history by transforming it into art. His quest is to save his life through the imaginative transformation of the mundane into the divine. The enabling symbol of this transformation is the spirit Ephraim, whose metamorphosis from a parlor game spirit into the daemonic representative of the sublime, who mediates between man and God, is described in "The Will" (SP 271). This poem is referred to in the beginning pages of *The Book of Ephraim* (CL 4) and serves as an informal preface to the trilogy.

Ephraim's transformation is initially resisted by the poet, who must be forced to accept Ephraim as a daemonic spirit, the conduit to God, which Merrill equates in this poem with the Jungian unconscious: "God and the Unconscious are one" (CL 74). JM's eventual acknowledgment of Ephraim as God's representative is a recognition of the unconscious will within the self. The quest to make conscious the unconscious will is a quest to know God and to accept the self's divinity. The acceptance of the individual unconscious as God implies an acknowledgment of the self's responsibility for its every action and desire. In "The Will," Merrill shows us how he was forced by his unconscious will, embodied in the figure of Ephraim, to accept this will as his own. This acceptance paves the way for JM's quest *into* the unconscious in an attempt to know the self and to "save the face" of God (SP 275). This quest is the subject of *The Book of Ephraim.*

The action of "The Will" is centered on a trip to a wedding to be held in a garden, which will be the setting for the poem's conclusion. The poem's beginning is set in a room with "coal black walls" in the "dead of winter" (SP 271). With these few facts in hand, we can correctly assume that the poem is in the form of a myth of deliverance, which moves from dark to light, from death to life, and from unknown to known.

In transit to the wedding, Merrill's manuscript for his novel is lost, forgotten in a taxi, along with his wedding gift, "an old wall-eyed stone-blond Ibis" (SP 273). Earlier in the poem, the poet hints that "ibis" refers to more than this statue when he recalls a dream in which he is wandering the streets of Paris. The dream figure comes upon "a façade he seemed to know / From times he'd seen it all aglow" (SP 271), but he finds no one at home:

> He rang impulsively. No bell
> Resounded from within the dark hotel.
>
> Its front door, Roman-numeralled,
> Still said "I" in white-on-emerald.

Some humbler way into the edifice
Was chalked just legibly "*Ibis*." (SP 271)

As Stephen Yenser has remarked, "I bis" is "the quasi-French address for a second self" (7). This shadowy self, along with the poet's acknowledged self represented by "I," have both grown unresponsive to the poet's conscious will; they refuse to answer the door.

The conscious will's impotence, in comparison to the poet's unconscious will, has increasingly dire consequences, which the poet details in the next sonnet, the third in the sequence of thirteen of which "The Will" is composed.

I'm at an airport, waiting. The scar itches.
Carving, last month I nearly removed my thumb.
Where was my mind? Lapses like this become
Standard practice. Not all of them leave me in stitches.

In growing puzzlement I've felt things losing
Their grip on me. What's done is done, dreamlike;
Clutches itself too late to stop the oozing
Reds, the numbing inward leak . . . (SP 272)

Merrill's use of the word "lapses" reminds us that, in psychological terms, an omission is never an accident but is the outward manifestation of the unconscious will. The poet gives further indication that he is under the control of such a hidden will by his adoption of the point of view of an objective, disinterested observer—as though these "lapses" were someone else's. He has not lost his grip on things; things have lost their grip on him.

But the crucial lapse, the forgetting of his novel together with the symbolic ibis in the taxi, is too important to be so easily disowned. The poet finds himself forced to admit that the manuscript did *not* forget him; he unconsciously willed its loss:

Gone for good. In the first shock of
Knowing it he tries
To play the dummy, dreads to advertise,
"Drinks water" like a character in Chekhov.

Life dims and parches. Self-inflicted
Desolation a faint horselaugh jars.
Property lies toppled, seeing stars
Nowhere in the dry dreambed reflected.

So that tonight's pint-size amphibian
Wriggler from murky impulse to ethereal act
Must hazard the dimensions of a man

Of means. Of meanings. Codicil
And heir alike. White-lipped survivor hacked
Out of his own Will. (SP 274)

If life is a play, then the poet's stage has been upset, with its "property" toppled and its "stars" missing. But the "pint-size amphibian," the poet's chameleon representative in this sonnet, proves that he is amenable to such swift changes of environment. The acceptance by the poet of both his impulse and his act, his willingness to call the action his own and to accept the consequences, "codicil and heir alike," allows him to be a "survivor."

The transformation of the unconscious will into conscious will is a moral victory and a sign of psychological maturity. Like "The Broken Home," "The Will" is a poem about psychic maturation. The lost ibis might be thought of as a symbol of the poet's younger, psychically immature, pre-Ephraim self. The poet writes, "I bought it with / A check my father wrote before his death" (SP 273), pointing to his own childlike status. The statue is lost on the way to a wedding, a literary convention used to symbolize the progress from childhood to adulthood.

The lost novel was the work of a psychically immature creator. Ephraim says to JM:

BY THE WAY SINCE U DID NOT CONSULT
THEIR SUBJECT YR GLUM PAGES LACKED HIS GLORY.
That stings. The guide and I lock horns like stags.
What is *his* taste? Aquinas? Bossuet? (SP 275)

Merrill's reference to Ephraim as "the guide" and his subsequent mentioning of "Aquinas," the maker of the "map" behind Dante's poem, indicates that he has begun to take his relation with this spirit more seriously than before. In the previous stanza, even, he had written of Ephraim:

we take you with a grain of salt,
Protagonist at best of the long story
Sketches and notes for which were my missing bag's
Other significant cargo, by the way. (SP 275)

What accounts for this about-face? With the novel's loss, Ephraim has suddenly become "the household heavyweight" (CL 23). His voice takes on authority:

SOIS SAGE DEAR HEART & SET MY TEACHINGS DOWN
Why, Ephraim, you belong to the old school—
You think the Word by definition good.

IF U DO NOT YR WORLD WILL BE UNDONE
& HEAVEN ITSELF TURN TO ONE GRINNING SKULL
So? We must write to save the face of God? (SP 275)

With this question, Merrill prepares the way for *The Book of Ephraim,* which is written both to save the face of God and to allow the poet to reach "the 'god' within" (REC 66). The quest to reach this god is an "old school" quest for the Word that will save both god and man, the Word that cannot be spoken but may be experienced as the sublime.

Merrill's quest for the sublime in *Ephraim* becomes possible only after the novel is abandoned and Ephraim is given a greater role in the self. The poet seems to be urging us to consider the lost novel in Jungian terms as a "projection" into fiction of the contradictions he has felt in himself between his conscious and unconscious wills. Such a projection results in an estrangement between the conscious self and the unconscious self, between what we choose to think of ourselves and what we, in fact, are.

Projections are false solutions to a difficult problem. They hide but do not solve the impasse between the unconscious and conscious selves. JM says in *The Book of Ephraim*: "I . . . imagined that the novel *was* / A step towards reality / . . . an effort to survey / The arteries of Ephraim's influence," but Ephraim insists that it was a step *away* from reality (CL 66). JM admits that he had tried to "isolate the subject from his environment"—which we might interpret as trying to project into the work of fiction the insoluble impasse between the conscious and unconscious wills that Ephraim represents within the poet's psyche—but argues that he did this in an effort to know himself: "I needed neutral ground . . . / Landscape and figures once removed, in glass," whereupon Ephraim responds, "TWICE REMOVED THANKS TO MY COUP DE GRACE" (CL 66).

Ephraim's action, representing the poet's unconscious will, is at once a death-blow to the lost novel (and the projected self it represents) and an act of grace. Without it, the poet would have continued projecting, hiding the schism between the conscious and unconscious, instead of striving for their reconciliation in the sublime union of the poem. Merrill's attempt to "explore the arteries of Ephraim's influence" in his novel is based on the assumption that Ephraim can be observed objectively without being recognized and accepted as a part of the self. Ephraim corrects this assumption in "The Will" by forcing JM to accept him as the representative of his unconscious will.

Although the poet is unwilling to accept Ephraim as a representative of this will in the lost novel, his portrayal of Ephraim in the novel as "Eros" indicates that he understands the divine nature of his familiar spirit. Plato explored the nature of Eros in *The Symposium,* which we may be certain Merrill has in mind from repeated references throughout the trilogy. When we read the poet's assertion that Ephraim/Eros exists in the area between the ideal and the real, "Between one floating realm unseen powers rule . . . / And one we feel is ours, and call the real" (CL 20), we can assume that he is aware of the implied reference to Plato's definition of the Greek god of love: "He [Eros] is a great spirit, and like all spirits he is intermediate between the divine and the mortal. . . . He interprets . . . between gods and men . . . he is the mediator who spans the chasm which divides them" (193). In Ephraim, Merrill discovers his Eros. Ephraim is a means to an end, the conjoining of the divine and mundane. But, like Eros, Ephraim may be misused and so become the source of damnation, taking "damnation" to be the opportunity for salvation that has been proffered but refused.

Merrill misuses Ephraim in the writing of his lost novel, in which he makes Ephraim/Eros responsible for every character's misery. In the novel, Eros represents the divine that punishes the mundane by offering a glimpse of an unreachable heaven. When Merrill recounts in section J of the trilogy how Ephraim resents this negative portrayal of his figure—"Ephraim scolds me for the lost novel's / Fire and brimstone version of his powers" (CL 33)—he implicitly accepts that the portrayal was unfair, that it was the result of his own reluctance to accept responsibility for the life history that the novel satirizes. The novel parodies the sublime instead of embracing it. Once accepted as a part of the self in "The Will," Ephraim/Eros is no longer seen as the source of the schism between the mundane and the divine, but rather as the healer of that rent.

With the acceptance of Ephraim in "The Will" as a representative of the unconscious, the poet is prepared to begin his unparodied quest for the sublime as described in *The Book of Ephraim*. In this poem, the negative, "unconsciously projected" elements of the lost novel are not abandoned. To do so would be to hide them, once again, from the view of the conscious self. Rather, the novel becomes a "sub-text" to the progression of the poem. Under Ephraim's guiding influence, the world is no longer seen as endangered and ever on the brink of dissolution, as in the lost novel. Once the poem is begun, we have entered the world of "the happy ending." The poem's existence is proof of JM's successful quest to become the poet of "The Book of Ephraim."

Two quests are in progress throughout *The Book of Ephraim*: the quest for the sublime and the quest to write a poem *about* the quest for the sublime—what we might call the quest for composition. We must keep the two quests separate in our minds and yet recognize that the quests are inseparable in the poem itself. They are dependent upon each other; one cannot succeed without the success of the other, and the failure of one necessitates the failure of the other.

In his quest for composition, JM must convince himself that this poem is worth writing. His reluctance to write the poem stems, in part, from his conviction that art negates life—that his devotion to poetry, and the quest for the sublime that this implies, will lessen his potential for other, more mundane commitments, such as his relationship with David Jackson (DJ). The argument that "art negates life" can be successfully answered only by the argument that art *enables* a richer, fuller life. The poet's devotion to the quest for the sublime makes other commitments more meaningful and even more "real."

The poet's devotion to the sublime does not fully account for his neglect of his relationships with others—at least, from *their* point of view. The poet alone receives the benefit of his commitment to the sublime quest, the immortality of his name as preserved by his work. One could argue that the poet's relations who find their way into this work are also immortalized, but this may not seem a fair reimbursement to those whose lives have been used as material for someone else's art, as DJ himself complains in *The Changing Light*.

The poet-quester has his own complaints about the quest for the sublime. He experiences first-hand the ultimate futility of the quest, the impossibility of ever fully preserving the sublime moment in art. From his point of view, the quest for this fleeting sublime seems endless. He is in danger of giving in to the vision of the absurd, glimpsed at the end of "The Book of Ephraim," which is caused by the endless repetition of his quest. The vision of the absurd would convince him that all of life is eternal recurrence—and, in this sense, "immortal"—and that man alone is out of synch, for wishing to stop the wheel from turning. The poet's wish to conquer time chains him to time and prevents him from experiencing eternity in every moment. The absurdist vision is the ironic reward the quester receives for his valiant but arrogant effort to save time lost. It is his punishment for having attempted to overturn the natural order.

The Book of Ephraim can be thought of as a single, sustained quest for the poem's composition, and for the sublime, and simultaneously as a series of individual quests. The poem consists of twenty-six sections, labeled from A to Z. We might consider the significance of such an ordering, as opposed to a numerical ordering (1 to 26). The numbering of sections implies accretion, as well as progression, whereas the lettering of sections implies that each section is given equal weight. We infer no inherent hierarchical distinction between the letters "D" and "V," whereas we clearly recognize that 4 is "less than" 22. It is only by placing several of the lettered sections together in order—"A, B, C, D," for example—that we understand that progression is implied.

Each section of *The Book of Ephraim* is concerned with one or more of the facets of the quest-romance, the search for the sublime. This is the poem's primary theme. The quest for composition is the poem's secondary theme. The quest for the sublime is repeated throughout the poem in many forms. In section F, the poet depicts the sublime quest, after the manner of "The Will," as being the story of the acceptance of the unconscious will as one's own. Section F is especially significant because of its retelling and revision of Shakespeare's *The Tempest,* one of the major subtexts in "The Book of Ephraim."

The Tempest is a natural work for Merrill to turn to in this poem. It is concerned with one of his major themes—the negation of reality that is implied in every creative effort—and the subsequent renunciation of art that is implied by the exhaustion of artistic effort and a return to the real world. *The Tempest* tells how the creative artist gains his power by temporarily subduing the two facets of the unconscious will: the physical, represented by Caliban, and the spiritual, represented by Ariel. Prospero's power over his enchanted isle, which we might label in Jungian terms his "projected unconscious," begins with his discovery of and victory over these two facets of the unconscious, Caliban and Ariel, the prior inhabitants of the island. The parallel to Prospero's victory in *The Book of Ephraim* is the poet's master/servant relationship with Ephraim, who has a "dual" nature analogous to that of Caliban/Ariel. Merrill's developing relationship with Ephraim, his "familiar spirit," leads him to the projected unconscious of the lost novel—this poem's parallel of Prospero's enchanted island.

When projected, the unconscious cannot be accepted as one's own. It may be recognized as such only when the self destroys its projection, abandons its "island" or "novel." Once Prospero abjures his rough magic and prepares to leave his island, he acknowledges that Caliban is Ariel's natural twin and part of his own will: "This thing of darkness I / Acknowledge mine" (5. 1. 275–76). The parallel passage in Merrill's poem "The Will" occurs when JM accepts that his lost novel's

Caliban—the Ephraim character, Eros—is the representative of his own unconscious will. The parallel passage in section F of *Ephraim* comes when JM acknowledges the section's Caliban character as his "kissing kin" (CL 19).

The Caliban character in section F is, paradoxically and crucially, a chimpanzee named "Miranda." According to Merrill's Jungian rendering of *The Tempest*, Miranda is Caliban transformed, accepted as the "thing of darkness" in one's unconscious will, and reintegrated into the conscious self. The poet's acknowledgement of this unconscious will, which allows for the transformation of Caliban into Miranda, takes place, fittingly enough, in a town called "Purgatory," the site of spiritual healing. The date of the transformation is April 1st, April Fool's Day, which we might take as evidence that the poet-quester has been a fool *not* to recognize Caliban as Miranda, not to have seen through her "skeptic, brooding mask" to the "child-face alight" beneath. JM asks, "Who / Can doubt she's one of us?" (CL 18). Accepting that she is indeed "one of us" allows for her re-naming from Caliban to Miranda. Such a renaming signifies a change in relation from slave to daughter—kissing kin.

Caliban's transformation into Miranda indicates a new role for the unconscious will in Merrill's poem. In *The Tempest*, Miranda prompts Prospero's action, as he himself assures her:

> I have done nothing but in care of thee,
> Of Thee my dear one, thee my daughter, who
> Art ignorant of what thou art. (1. 2. 16–18)

Miranda is the whole of which Caliban and Ariel are merely halves. They are slaves, projections of Prospero's unconscious will. The creator's duty to these slaves is that of the master to his servants, to punish and reward. The relationship is one-sided. The projecting creator "rules" his island, or novel, but does not feel responsible for its inhabitants' actions, motives, and desires. By contrast Prospero feels an overwhelming sense of responsibility for his "ignorant" daughter. This sense leads him to lament the poverty of his exile from reality. On his projected island he is no more to her than "master of a full poor cell / And thy no great father" (1. 2. 20–21).

Miranda represents the potential for harmony made possible by the destruction of the unconscious will's projections. She is the symbol of the idealized, harmonious relationship between the conscious and the unconscious, the mundane and the divine, the physical and the spiritual. It is for the sake of this ideal world of harmony and love—as opposed to his island-cell of judgment, slavery, and punishment—that Prospero "abjures" his "rough magic" (5. 1. 50–51). In the same sense, JM accepts that his novel's "loss" was the necessary prelude to his quest for the sublime. This quest is made possible by the transformation of Ephraim from Caliban to Miranda.

The fact that JM calls his island "Miranda's," and never "Caliban's," indicates to the reader that the poet's mission there has been successful. The poet, looking back in reflection as he writes, can recognize the island as "Miranda's" only after he has gained a vision of wholeness made possible through his acceptance of the unconscious will, represented by the beast Caliban. We are again reminded that *Ephraim* is a dual quest; the success of the quest for composition, which is proven to be successful by the poem in hand, is also proof of the success of the quest for the sublime, which begins with the acceptance of the unconscious will, the transformation of Caliban into Miranda.

In his version of *The Tempest*, Merrill places the chimpanzee Miranda on an island as part of an experiment in which she is being raised by humans *as* a human. In the final stage of the experiment, Miranda will be bred with another chimpanzee to "determine what / Traces, if any, she will then transmit / To her own offspring, of our mother wit" (CL 18). If we take Miranda to represent the unconscious, or id, then we may take the human scientists who are raising her to be representatives of the ego. We can understand their effort to "humanize" the primitive as a symbol of the general work of civilization as Freud defined it in his famous conclusion to "The Dissection of the Psychical Personality," "Where id was, there ego shall be. It is a work of culture—not unlike the draining of the Zuider Zee" (NIL 100). JM recognizes that his quest is to overcome the "instinctual" obstacles that the unconscious poses to knowledge and happiness. He wants to make the unconscious a participant in his conscious will:

> Weren't we still groping, like Miranda, toward
> Some higher level?—subjects in a vast
> Investigation whose objective cast,
> Far from denying temperament, indeed
> Flung it like caution to the winds, like seed. (CL 19)

JM's unconscious will is both subject and object in this quest for self. When he refuses to deny temperament, the very core of the unconscious self, but flings it like seed into the world, he is seeking a connection between inner and outer realities, between divine and mortal, unconscious and conscious. He is attempting to save God's "face" (SP 275) by giving the unconscious will a human visage.

Alert readers of Merrill's early work will have foreseen this quest to "save the face of God" in the poet's pronounced tendency to "animate" inanimate objects, to spiritualize the material, and materialize the spiritual. His household furnishings, such as a table, lamp, paperweight, and mirror, are all "inhabited," as are the figures of the landscape. "The Black Mesa" speaks to its surrounding plain as to an old and unfaithful lover (SP 217). "The Banks of a Stream" plead with the water flowing through it (SP 210). And "The Waterfall" urges all who hear, "While I live / Come live within me" (SP 249). The poet is alert to the very stones crying out for life. In these poems, he exhibits the magic of Prospero releasing Ariel from the pine (*The Tempest* 1. 2. 293).

Like Prospero, the poet may be endangered by his powers if he uses them not to expand his vision of reality but to isolate himself by assuming a false position above reality. From such a position of false superiority, he may come to believe that, instead of hearing the waterfall's urging, he *causes* it to urge, just as he makes the banks of the stream plead. Prospero's severed relations with Caliban prove him guilty of such pride. He has sought to rule over nature instead of being content with his supreme position within the natural order.

JM's affront to the natural order comes directly after his successful meeting with the chimpanzee, Miranda, in which he recognizes his relation to her primitive nature and acknowledges the unconscious, instinctual will she represents in himself. Having recognized the limitless will of the unconscious as his own, he appears to make the mistake of allowing this will to dominate his view of the world—to separate him from the "reality principle" that would indicate to him the impossibility of completely fulfilling the desires of the unconscious will. This mistake is made manifest in his efforts at "genetic engineering."

In the cosmic system of reincarnation that Ephraim describes, other-worldly figures serve as "patrons" for people in this world, who are their representatives. Ephraim expresses frustration with his recent representatives, who have been weak or badly cared for and have died early. JM and DJ suggest to Ephraim that he consider two pregnant friends of theirs who could provide stable homes for his earthly representatives. Ephraim takes them up on their offer and slips "THE SOULS / LIKE CORRESPONDENCE INTO PIGEONHOLES" (CL 20). With their success, JM and DJ feel they have "achieved . . . / At last some kind of workable relation / Between the two worlds. Had bypassed religion. . . . / Had left heredity, Narcissus bent / Above the gene pool" (CL 20). And yet, in section I, they are reproved for their actions. "We have MEDDLED," JM reports, "And the POWERS / ARE FURIOUS" (CL 29). Their punishment is the loss of Ephraim, whom they fail to contact, "hard as we've tried" (CL 29), on the Ouija board.

The questers have tried to gain concrete proof of Ephraim's existence by orchestrating the birth of his human representatives. But the sublime that Ephraim represents is unprovable. It may be experienced only in the sublime moment of intersection between our time-bound world and the timeless. Remembering that Ephraim's name in the novel is Eros, we recall that, in the Eros/Psyche myth, the god of love departs the moment that Psyche recognizes him. This is the nature of the sublime. To attempt to hold it is to lose it.

Outside of the sublime moment, the existence of the sublime must be taken on faith. Ephraim himself stresses this when he tells JM and DJ that "DEVOTION" leads the way to God (CL 59). JM's and DJ's attempt to dictate reality, in order to gain the "feather of proof" (CL 258) of Ephraim's existence through the birth of his representatives to their friends, is a betrayal of trust and shows a lack of faith in their familiar spirit. Ephraim himself leads them into this error, but he abandons them when they fail to recognize their action *as* an error, scaring him with "flippancies" (CL 29) when he warns them of their mistake.

In quest-romance terms, this entire scenario may be viewed as a test for the questers, a "trial" prompted by Ephraim, the questers' unconscious will, which they momentarily fail. Their pride leads them to believe that they can direct this limitless will toward their limited ends. They seek proof of Ephraim's existence, feeling:

> So thoroughly exempted from ideal
> Lab conditions as to stride roughshod
> Past angels all agape, and pluck the weird
> Sister of Things to Come by her white beard. (CL 19)

The questers of this passage consider themselves superior to the sublime moment in which the "ideal" is merged with the "lab conditions" of our mutable world. By claiming to be "exempted from" the sublime, they imply that there is no distinction between the mundane and the divine. In their pride, they "stride roughshod / Past angels all agape," implicitly questioning the existence or necessity of "agape," divine love, of which Eros/Ephraim is the representative. By doubting Ephraim/Eros and demanding proof of his existence, the questers feel that they can either disprove the existence or "bridge over" the chasm between the divine and the mundane in one glorious movement. But they succeed only in hiding the chasm from view. They lose sight of divinity in their attempt to contain and explain it.

JM's visit to his "ex-shrink" (CL 29), to whom he tells the whole story of how he and DJ were scolded for their meddling and of Ephraim's subsequent disappearance, is proof of the questers' failure. By seeking the higher authority of the analyst, JM implicitly denies the authenticity of his familiar spirit. This is made clear when the analyst encourages JM to "explain away" Ephraim using Freudian psychological theory. The analyst would have JM believe that Ephraim is a psychological projection, developed in response to his and DJ's combined guilt for being "sons who have not sired a child." The analyst condescendingly asks, "can you find no simpler ways / To sound each other's depths of spirit?" (CL 30).

JM's faith in Ephraim is shaken but not destroyed by his trip to the analyst. That night, he tries to make contact through the Ouija board and is successful. Ephraim returns to the questers as the reward for their continued belief and their constancy in the face of doubts. Having won Ephraim back, the poet decides that he must accept him henceforth without proof:

> The point—one twinkling point by now of thousands—
> Was never to forego, in favor of
> Plain dull proof, the marvelous nightly pudding. (CL 32)

Despite his questionable credentials, Ephraim is leading the questers to greater knowledge of themselves and is adding an irreplaceable dimension to their quotidian existence—one that the self-limiting, rational mind cannot fathom:

> If he had blacked out reason (or vice versa)
> On first sight, we instinctively avoided
> Facing the eclipse with naked eye.
> . . . .
> Like Tosca hadn't we
> Lived for art and love? We were not tough-
> Or literal-minded, or unduly patient
> With those who were. (CL 31)

It is typical of Merrill's engagingly reticent and self-deprecating manner that he puts himself in the lowly company of the opera heroine, when he could just as well have written: Like Dante, had we not lived for love? Or like Proust, had we not lived for art? Similarly, the clever eclipse metaphor, used to represent the repudiation of reason, disguises the crucial nature of this act. The repudiation of reason opens up the mind to the instinctual and irrational unconscious that Ephraim represents and that Merrill equates, via Jung, with God. The repudiation of reason is not the behavior of an indolent, cowardly, or specious mind—as Merrill's arch tone seems to imply—but an act of faith and of devotion to things not seen or heard.

When the questers attempt to gain proof of Ephraim's existence, they make the same error that Merrill implies was Yeats' when dealing with *his* familiar spirit, Leo Africanus. Yeats forced his revelations into a "workable" system, cementing the "relation / Between the two worlds" (CL 20). Yeats is the great "occultist" figure in modern English-language poetry. Merrill implies that Yeats' *A Vision,* that "maze of inner logic, dogma, dates" (CL 14) that resulted from his occultist experiences with Leo Africanus, is flawed by excessive *reasoning*. Its complexity is proof of the author's distrust of his material. Ephraim seems to support this opinion when he says of Yeats' extremely complicated system: "POOR OLD YEATS / STILL SIMPLIFYING" (CL 14). The implication is that no system, regardless of its complexity, can replace the individual familiar spirit as a conveyor of the irreducible and contradictory nature of the sublime. The truest symbol of the sublime is individual human nature, which is both divine and mundane. Yeats' refusal to admit Leo Africanus into his work as a character in his own right is taken by Merrill as proof of the elder poet's failure to believe in his own vision.

JM's doubting of Ephraim is not only bad faith but bad manners. This is a serious error for Merrill, for whom "good" manners are at the very heart of good morals and true art. He says of manners: "Someone who does not take them seriously is making a serious mistake" (REC 33). Throughout *The Book of Ephraim,* JM is obsessed with the possibility that bad manners are required of the poet who uses his life as material for art. This is not a new obsession for the poet. In *The (Diblos) Notebook,* the narrator/author abandons his novel rather than be faced with the record of his creative aggression, his use of those around him as metaphors for art. The poet of "Ephraim" might be thought of as a judge who is weighing use against devotion. He is striving to convince himself that use in any form is an act of devotion, that it is therefore life-affirming and ultimately "good." If he succeeds in proving to himself that use and devotion are inseparable in this mutable world, then he can proceed to write his poem using his life as material. If he cannot accept the interdependent relationship of use and devotion, then he presumably will be forced to abandon his poem, as the narrator of *Diblos* abandons his novel, since he is unwilling to accept as his own the aggression-through-creation necessary for its making.

Much of the argument over the issue of use and devotion is recorded in the bits and pieces of the lost novel that find their way into the finished poem. This novel is an example of the author's having attempted to use art as a vantage point from which to condemn life. All of the main characters in the lost novel are in competition, either with one another or with the environment itself. None is allowed to strive for the sublime, represented in the figure of Eros (Ephraim), without injury to himself or others. Many of the novel's characters metamorphose into characters taken from "real life" whom Merrill uses for "The Book of Ephraim." These translated characters are less obviously self-centered than their originals in the novel. When they use one another, they are more likely to have justifiable reasons. Those who are users in the poem are also used in one way or another. In general, we find the finished poem's moral landscape to be much less black and white than that in the lost novel.

In the lost novel, villains and heroes fall into separable and opposing camps. In this survival-of-the-fittest environment, the very presence of Eros is a reproof. It is fitting that this God's unlooked-for arrival is the work of the novel's most disturbing figure, Joanna, who arrives in the novel's setting in the desert Southwest carrying a "gift-wrapped Ouija board" (CL 35). Merrill describes Joanna in section J of *Ephraim*:

> Joanna (Chapter One) sat in the plane,
> Smoke pouring from her nostrils. Outside, rain;
> Sunset; mild azure; sable bulks awince
> With fire—and all these visible at once
> While Heaven, quartered like a billionaire's
> Coat of arms, put on stupendous airs.
> Earth lurched and shivered in the storm's embrace
> But kept her distances, lifting a face
> Unthinkingly dramatic in repose
> As was Joanna's. Desiccated rose
> Light hot on bone, ridge, socket where the streak
> Of glancing water—if a glance could speak—
> Said, "Trace me back to some loud, shallow, chill,
> Underlying motive's overspill." (CL 33)

Joanna is an infernal figure; she is surrounded by smoke and fire. But she is also surrounded by sunset and mild azure. She stands in the novel for Jung's "destructive anima" (CL 35). The poet's description of her makes her seem both destructive and dangerous: her motives are loud, shallow, and chill. But she is also compared to Earth itself, our archetypal mother, and she is implicitly compared to the damsel in distress as she lurches and shivers in the "storm's embrace."

She is the manifestation of a typically dual Jungian archetype. She can work either for or against an individual, depending upon his attitude toward what she represents—the eternal feminine. This feminine archetype, or anima, is seen by the male psyche as either destructive or loving. She is the overwhelming mother and treacherous lover figure, the wicked stepmother and femme fatale of myth. She is likewise the protective and loving mother and the endangered virginal bride. In the quest for the sublime, what Jung calls the quest for psychic individuation, she may be the source of strength, the protective mother and muse, the representative of the goal to be attained, the damsel in distress who needs rescuing. Alternatively, she may be the vicious opponent to that quest, the dragon of myth, and the insidious destroyer of the quester's will, the femme fatale.

In the lost novel, she is consistently destructive, an obstacle to be overcome. But the fact that she introduces Eros into the other characters' lives is proof of her potential for good. The positive anima is represented in the novel by an equally imposing but more attractive female character, Rosamund Smith. Mrs. Smith appears on the scene as the result of Joanna's "rout" (CL 71), by which we are given to understand that she is Joanna "transformed." Rosamund Smith is the novel's true heroine. The poet describes her in his list of dramatis personae.

> "Smith, Rosamund," character in the novel,
> Later the Marchesa Santofior.
> Perennially youthful, worldly, rich,
> And out of sight until the close. (CL 13)

Mrs. Smith, who is given scant attention in the bits of the novel that remain in "Ephraim," plays a critical role in the poem's conclusion, where she is referred to in her mythical guise as the benevolent mother figure, the "ancient, ageless woman of the world" (CL 92). In section S, we are given proof of Mrs. Smith's archetypal character when she is described as the "resourceful Mrs. Smith . . . / Who with a kiss flew off to marry myth" (CL 67). In the novel, as in the poem, she is out of sight until the close. Her appearance represents the quester's victory over the destructive anima, which has opposed the quest for the sublime but, when "transformed," becomes the enabling muse. Merrill represents this transformation as the death and birth of a "rose"; the "desiccated rose," Joanna, turns into the "perennially youthful" *Rosamund* Smith.

The poet gives us several variations throughout the poem of the archetypal struggle between the questing hero and the destructive anima. In section Q, we find a "camp" version of the transformation of the anima. The poet quotes in this section from an imaginary writer, A. H. Clarendon, who tells the story of an American serviceman who is "behaving quite outrageously" in a bar "late in the war." An American admiral is "incensed" by the serviceman's behavior and demands his "name and squadron," whereupon the serviceman, Teddie "snapped shut his thin gold compact (from Hermes) and narrowed his eyes at the admiral. 'My name,' he said distinctly, 'is Mrs. Smith'" (CL 58). "Hermes," like Ephraim/Eros, is a daemonic spirit who mediates between the human and the divine. Teddie's "compact" from Hermes is proof of his status as a quester for the sublime; his adopted feminine persona, "Mrs. Smith," is proof that he has won the battle with his destructive anima, which, once defeated, is integrated into the self, as the defeated Joanna is transformed into JM's interior paramour and muse.

Merrill figures the successful ego-quester throughout the poem as a fey male. The quester's "feminine" sexuality serves as proof of his successful integration of the feminine anima. In the lost novel, the character "Sergei" stands for the successful quester, whose role it is to lead the novice quester, Leo, to the sublime. Sergei is one of the first of the novel's characters to "take up" Eros/Ephraim: "Sergei, their queer / Neighbor uphill, whom every seventh year / Some unseemly passion overthrows, / Adds him [Eros] to a list of Tadzio's" (CL 47). That Sergei is a successful quester is proven by his ability to tutor Leo in his quest.

We have been given further proof of Sergei's successful quest for self-revelation earlier in the novel when the author describes how Sergei experiences a "miracle." The miracle occurs when he revisits a holy spot in the Southwest and finds that it has been transformed; "a pit of wonder-working clay / Beyond the altar" that supposedly healed cripples is gone, and "the very crosses" have "turned to stone" (CL 34). Looking at the transformed landscape, Sergei would "have the feeling / He too was cured, refurbished, on his way" (CL 34). The "transformed" landscape is representative of a positive change within Sergei's psyche. We have seen an example of such an "outward" manifestation of an "inner" transformation in "The Will," where the black room of the beginning stanza is "transformed" into the garden of the poem's conclusion, reflecting the successful quest by JM to reintegrate his unconscious will into his conscious self.

Also serving as proof of Sergei's cured status is the fact that he can see through Joanna's "smoke-screen" to the destructive archetype beneath. Joanna and Sergei meet at the site of the transformed clay-pit and

> "Recognize" each other, or I as author
> Recognize in them the plus and minus
> —Good and evil, let my reader say—
> Vital to the psychic current's flow.
> Joanna worries me. (Sergei I know.) (CL 35)

Merrill *would* know Sergei, for in the novel Sergei represents the "positive" version of the authorial self whose job it is to save the "negative" version of the self represented by Leo.

In order to keep straight all of these "versions" of the singular poetic self, we might look to Jung's figuration of the psyche that Merrill seems to be using. According to Jung, the psyche is fourfold, comprised of a positive and negative feminine archetype, as well as a positive and negative masculine archetype. We have already labeled Joanna as the negative feminine archetype in the novel and Mrs. Smith as the positive. We can now add Leo as the negative masculine archetype and Sergei as his positive counterpart. These four characters in the novel represent four facets of the creator's psyche, each of whom plays a specific role in the self. In the singular male psyche, the negative feminine archetype (the destructive anima) serves as nemesis. In order to be psychically healthy or whole, the male quester seeks to recognize this archetype, identifying the figures in real life onto whom he has projected his fear and hatred of the feminine nature within himself. By admitting responsibility for these projections, he can come to terms with the feminine nature within.

In Jung's system of archetypes, the unconscious is feminine and the conscious is masculine. The male psyche's struggle to accept the feminine within himself is analogous to the questing self's struggle—as seen in "The Will" and in this poem's version of *The Tempest*—to accept and take responsibility for his unconscious self. The male psyche, or conscious self, which does *not* accept its feminine counterpart, the unconscious, becomes dominated by the negative male archetype. The male whose psyche is dominated by this negative archetype is characteristically defensive in the face of the feminine unconscious. His defensiveness may be acted out as aggression against this unconscious feminine self. To this feminine-dominated male, the fellow male who is at peace with his unconscious feminine nature appears as an ideal to be either worshiped or scorned. If the feminine-dominated male allows this positive version of himself to be adopted as a goal, then he may achieve transformation, himself becoming dominated by the positive male archetype. He will have bridged the gap between his masculine and feminine natures, the conscious and the unconscious. In quest-romance terms, we would say that he achieves a vision of the sublime in which the time-bound conscious self intersects with the immortal unconscious, the eternal feminine.

In the lost novel, Leo is dominated by the negative archetypes; his conscious and unconscious wills are estranged. He is seeking to become a representative of the positive archetypes, a quester after the sublime. His psychic health is threatened by his rebellion against his unconscious feminine nature. His friendship with Sergei, the novel's older and successful quester, offers hope of a "cure." Joanna, the negative feminine character in the lost novel, serves as the symbol of Leo's rebelliousness against the feminine in himself.

That the positive masculine archetype of Sergei and the negative feminine archetype of Joanna are struggling for domination of Leo is made clear by the relationship of all three characters to Eros, the daemonic god of transformation. Merrill figures the complicated relationship among these characters by placing Sergei and Joanna "at the Ouija board," which only works when they are "side by side" with Sergei's "Fingertips touching hers— / That woman, smoking, auburn-haired, abhorred" (CL 67). Leo transcribes the sessions with Eros. Leo's neutral placement between Sergei and Joanna indicates his precarious psychical balance.

That Leo begins his quest in a state of servitude to the destructive feminine is proven by his unhealthy relationship with his young wife. He uses Eros to punish his wife. He uses the representative of the ideal to punish the real, rather than seeking their conjoining in the sublime. When we first meet Leo, he is still "suffering" from his stint in Vietnam, although he has supposedly been "rehabilitated" (CL 48). This rehabilitation seems to have worked to "cover up" whatever Leo's personality had been to such an extent that his wife, Ellen, feels "she can neither reach nor exorcise / This Leo," whose "Clear gray eyes / Set in that face emotion has long ceased / To animate (except as heat waves do / A quarry of brown marble) give no clue" (CL 48). This Leo should remind us of the distant poet in "The Will" who has gradually "felt things losing / Their grip" on him (SP 272), and of "James" who is described in "The Thousand and Second Night" as an "unfeeling monster" (SP 97), prompting his friend's complaints:

"You were nice, James. . . . Or so

> I thought. But you have changed. I know, I know,
> People do change. Well, I'm surprised, I'm pained." (SP 96)

If these comparisons do not convince us that Leo is meant to represent the creative artist in his solipsism, then we have only to read further to find proof. Leo is intent on becoming a creator:

> Now he [Leo] wants their baby born
> As Eros's new representative.
> What *is* it when the person that you live
> With, live for, no longer—? (CL 48)

Remembering that Eros is Ephraim's name in the novel, we can see how Merrill is creating a parallel between JM's and DJ's effort to place Ephraim's souls into the "pigeonholes" of their pregnant friends and Leo's effort to impregnate his wife for the sake of Eros. In this fictional rendering, Merrill makes it clear that when an artist confuses art and life, the divine and the mundane, to such a degree, he transgresses on both.

Leo's treatment of Ellen is proof of his confusion and of his aggression. He has turned their bedroom into a stage with "music" and "glistening jellies" where the couple give "nightly / Performances whose choreography / Eros dictates and, the next day, applauds" (CL 48). Ellen feels both "distaste and fright" in the face of Eros. She

> struggles to dismiss
> As figment of their common fancy this
> Tyrannical ubiquitous voyeur
> Only to feel within her the child stir. (CL 48)

This is the closest JM comes in the trilogy to admitting that he might be using DJ unfairly for the writing of his poem. It is perhaps the most distasteful if, in one sense, most accurate portrait of the creator in all of Merrill's work. Each creator is a Prospero directing the enormous will-to-power of the unconscious (Eros or Ephraim, the tyrannical ubiquitous voyeur) toward his selfish ends, whether the creation of an island cell, a child, or a poem.

Leo's implied justification for his aggressive behavior toward Ellen is that he is a quester for the sublime in the service of Eros. He is seeking to create a baby worthy to be "Eros's new representative" (CL 48). He wants to gain some tangible proof of his relationship with Eros. That he might be sacrificing control over his own life and the stability of his marriage seems of little consequence to this quester who has undertaken a mission in the service of a god:

And Leo feels? Why, just that Eros knows.
Goes wherever they go. Watches. Cares.
Lighthearted, light at heart. A candle
Haloing itself, the bedroom mirror's
Wreath of scratches fiery-fine as hairs
(Joanna closes *Middlemarch* downstairs)
Making sense for once of long attrition. (CL 48)

Like Dorothea in George Eliot's novel, Leo feels drawn to the light of an ideal, whose candle will allow him to make sense of his disordered, mutable existence. He seeks divinity, striving to turn life's losses, "the fiery-fine" scratches on life's mirror, into a halo, a wreath about the head to signify how nothing, through striving after Love, can come to something, "making sense for once of long attrition."

Sublime moments such as these, although central to the self's well-being, do not make the self inviolate when faced with the world of daily existence. Indeed, the quester after the sublime owes this world a greater debt than his neighbor, who asks for and receives less. Leo "Can feel his crippling debt to—to the world— / Hearth where the night-long village of desire / Shrieks and drowns in automatic fire" (CL 48). Leo's desire for the sublime prompts his aggressive demands on those around him, whom he uses and discards as routinely as the phoenix is born and dies. Leo sacrifices his wife nightly for Eros's pleasure (which we cannot help but read as "JM uses DJ every evening to talk to Ephraim on the Ouija board"). Leo hopes that this behavior will culminate in the birth of something more lasting than the phoenix passion of desire—a child or a poem.

Before the child or poem can be born as a legitimate representative of the sublime, the creator must come to terms with the "crippling" aggression that is prompting and enabling its making. Otherwise the created child will be disfigured, like JM's lost novel. Such a child is the heir not of the sublime but of the creator's defensiveness when faced with evidence of his aggression-through-creation. In the lost novel, Leo must pay back his "crippling debt" to "the world" in order to be "healed." He must make amends for his aggression against the "natural order," symbolized by his destructive relationship with Ellen, before he himself will be well again and before his child can be born as Eros' representative.

Leo's effort to create Eros's representative, like every creative act, is an aggressive act against the natural order. By such an act, the creator makes a space for the self in the hostile world. His creation provides him with a mirror in which he can see himself as real, a part of the reality of creation. Taken to an extreme, this mirrored self grows to fill the entire world, until all of creation reflects its lineaments. At this point, the creating self can no longer distinguish between self and other. Like Prospero on his island, he will have subjected all of reality to his will, only to find himself a prisoner in his self-created "cell." Once this happens, the only creative act left is self-immolation, the destruction of the mirrored self, as when Prospero drowns his book. By such an act, the creating self releases reality from the boundaries of his limited will.

Leo figuratively relinquishes his will when he goes behind a waterfall in a symbolic act of self-immolation and purification:

> Stepping through it drenched, he finds himself
> On the far side of reflection, a deep shelf
> Hidden from the nakedest of eyes.
> Asked where he is, Eros must improvise
> HE IS WITH ME The others panic—dead?
> In fact (let this be where the orgies led) (CL 49)

Leo's movement to the "far side of reflection" indicates to us that he has given over control of his conscious, "reflective" will to the unconscious will, represented by Eros/Ephraim. From within the waterfall, "beyond reflection" (beyond the control of the self-justifying conscious self), the nightly "orgies" with Ellen may be seen as psychological projections, the manifestations of Leo's unwillingness to take responsibility for his desires and actions, which he has claimed to be "dictated" by Eros. When Leo goes behind the falls, he is given an opportunity to accept the unconscious self that Eros represents and that he has denied ever since his unexplained trauma in Vietnam. Behind the waterfall, this unconscious self materializes and is recognized by Leo as his "double" and his accuser:

> Leo in tears is kneeling by the bones
> He somehow knew would be there. Human ones.
> A seance can have been devoted to
> That young Pueblo, dead these hundred years,
> Whose spirit SEEKS REPOSE (One of the others
> Has killed him in a previous life? *Yes.*)
> Whose features Leo now hallucinates:
> Smooth skin, mouth gentle, eyes expressionless—
> The "spy" his outfit caught, one bamboo-slender
> Child ringed round by twenty weary men—
> Expressionless even when Leo—even when— (CL 49)

Leo's murder of the child in Vietnam causes a schism within the self whereby the conscious self defensively contends—as does JM at the beginning of "The Will"—that its thoughts and deeds are not its own, that it is a slave to an unknown will. Leo journeys behind the waterfall in an effort to rediscover this unknown will. His hallucination in which he brings his victim back to life allows him to relive the decisive moment of his aggression in which he killed not only his young victim but also that part of himself that took the victim's side. Having recognized his aggression, he can choose to deny that it is his own, thereby furthering the schism within the self between the conscious and unconscious, or he can accept his aggression and make amends by taking responsibility for his actions. That he does make amends through the divine power of Eros may be seen when "Sleep overtakes him clasping what he loathes / And loves, the dead self dressed in his own clothes" (CL 49). The schism within the self has been healed.

Having accepted the will of the feminine unconscious as his own, Leo is able to see the representative of the "negative" feminine, Joanna, as the destructive force she truly is. Joanna is "routed" and "jets / Back where she came from, through a sky in flames" (CL 71). The flames, like those in *Götterdämmerung* to which the poet alludes, represent the ending of a mythical cycle, the withdrawal of an old god, enabling the birth of a new one. The birth of Leo's little boy symbolizes the beginning of a new order (CL 71).

Leo's quest to be healed in the lost novel is the most elaborate version of the quest-romance cycle in "The Book of Ephraim," apart from the quest of JM himself. We might profitably think of Leo's quest as the precursor to JM's, since the poet's losing of his novel leads directly to the writing of this poem. All of the major elements of the quest for the sublime that JM undergoes are present, at least in embryo form, in Leo's quest.

The quest begins with Leo's "trauma" in Vietnam. This is tantamount to the "fall" from grace with which each quest cycle begins, the fall into the divided psyche of the mutable world. All of Merrill's poems that may be labeled as versions of the quest-romance begin with the recounting of this schism-producing fall. The poem "Log" begins with the flame forking "like a sudden path" (SP 189). In "Prism," an invisible wall is described as being "put up in mid-stride" (SP 64), prompting an ambiguous separation between in and out. In "The Broken Home," a window separates the narrator from the ideal family unit (SP 109). And in "The Will," the opening dream sequence recounts the alienation of the dreaming self from the "I" of reality (SP 271).

In its most basic form, this estranging fall is analogous to birth itself, the trauma by which we all enter this time-bound world. Merrill implicitly recognizes that time is the quester's nemesis when he quotes from Edmund Spenser's description of the Garden of Adonis: "But were it not, that *Time* their troubler is, / All that in this delightfull Gardin growes, / Should happie be, and haue immortal blis" (CL 61). The fall into the mutable world sets the quest in motion. From this point on, the quester is seeking to heal the rent within the self (and the world) between the ideal and the real, the divine and the mundane, the unconscious and the conscious, which is caused by time. Merrill figures the quester in this beginning stage as being either psychologically handicapped or physically ill. In order to be healed, the quester is forced to use those around him. We are not strong enough to heal ourselves. Time is seen as being responsible for human aggression and competition, since all aggression is ultimately caused by our struggle against death.

Up to this point, what we are calling the quest-romance cycle is applicable to all of us, since we have all experienced the trauma of birth whereby we fall into this world of existence, and since we all use one another in our struggle to make ourselves more content. But the next step in the quest cycle, the devotion to an ideal, sets apart those who are truly questers from those who are not. Ephraim makes a contrast between the questers and the non-questers (who, presumably, occupy two camps in heaven) in section Q: "SO FEW UP HERE WISH TO THINK THEIR EYES ARE TURNED HAPPILY UP AS THEY FLOAT TOWARD THE CLIFF   I WANT TO DO MORE THAN RIDE & WEAR & WAIT" (CL 60). He claims that "DEVOTION" separates the questers who are striving to make sense of their journey from the non-questers, who are floating ignorantly along on the current of existence. Through devotion, "TO EACH OTHER TO WORK TO REPRODUCTION TO AN IDEAL," we "ARRIVE AT GOD" (CL 59).

If we take "God," as Merrill seems to do, to mean "man at his best, fulfilling his greatest and most 'good' potential," then we can see how Ephraim is arguing that a world without devotion (an example of which is the world of the lost novel, with the exception of Sergei's devotion to Leo and Leo's devotion to Eros) is a world in which man is at his worst, struggling against his fellow man in an existence that is ruled by the base standard of the survival of the fittest. Ephraim does not deny that we live in such a world but implicitly argues that if we *must* use one another, then we should temper use with devotion.

Devotion mitigates the harmful effects of power. One way of reading *The Book of Ephraim* is to see it as the outward manifestation of the struggle within the psyche between the regressive urge to use power in a purely aggressive fashion and the opposing urge to devote oneself to a person, art-form, or ideal in order to direct and shape one's aggression. In the realm of undirected and unmitigated power (as this poem defines it), the aggressor does not recognize his victim or even admit his aggression. In the modern world at large, the symbol for this "naked" power is atomic energy, which, according to Merrill's figuring, negates all relationship, particularly the one between man and nature, and which leads to the loss of the self—what Ephraim calls the "SOUL"—whose existence cannot be known except through the cooperation of a reflecting environment:

> NO SOULS CAME FROM HIROSHIMA U KNOW
> EARTH WORE A STRANGE NEW ZONE OF ENERGY
> Caused by? SMASHED ATOMS OF THE DEAD MY DEARS
> News that brought into play our deepest fears. (CL 55)

In *Mirabell*, Merrill will define atomic energy as the negation of the integrity of matter. On the personal level, neglect leads to the loss of the "sense of self" on the part of both the neglecter and the neglected. In the opposing sphere of devotion, one is always performing the role of either the user or the used; both imply commitment. The neglecting self refuses to participate—or, rather, to *admit* of participation in the user-used relationship. The refusal to admit of a relationship to an "other," whether to an immaterial ideal or to a human relationship, will eventually lead the quester to feel that he is an unreal figure in a hostile world, as Merrill illustrates when describing his on-again, off-again relationship with Ephraim:

> This (1970) was the one extended
> Session with Ephraim in two years.
> (Why? No reason—we'd been busy living,
> Had meant to call, but never quite got round . . .)
> The cup at first moved awkwardly, as after
> An illness or estrangement. Had he missed us?
> YES YES emphatically. We felt the glow
> Of being needed, then a breath of frost,
> For if, poor soul, he did so, he was lost.
> Ah, so were we! (CL 55)

The neglected soul is a "poor soul," negated by its unresponsive and unreflecting environment. The soul that neglects, refusing to invest itself in another, will also find itself impoverished, having lost the reflecting other that makes the self feel secure and whole by connecting it to the world around it.

Investment of the self in the external world forges a link between inner and outer realities, between one's "ideal" inner world and the "real" external world. Bringing the two together is the goal of the quest for the sublime upon which poets embark when they attempt to create an exterior self on the page that mirrors the interior imaginative self. Lovers become questers when they seek to find a beloved who will correspond to their interior, idealized love.

In the mythical quest cycle with which we have been dealing, the quester's devotion is invested in a threatened loved object. This loved object—whether it be a sick king who requires a grail to be healed, a damsel who needs rescuing from a dragon, or a spirit like Ephraim who wants a poem to be born as its representative—is a symbol of the divided self (in Jungian terms), the self in which the conscious and unconscious are estranged from one another. The capture of the grail, the slaying of the dragon, and the birth of the child all represent successful conclusions of the quest, the healing of the schism within the quester's own psyche.

Before this schism can be healed, the quester must reach the sublime moment of revelation in which the mundane confronts the divine, in which the conscious self recognizes the unconscious self as its double. At this point, the quester is faced with a choice: He may accept the "double," unconscious self as his own, thereby accepting responsibility for his every desire and action. Alternatively, he may deny his relationship to this unconscious self, thereby perpetuating the schism within the self that causes him pain. In the lost novel, Leo's acceptance of the "dead self dressed in his own clothes" (CL 49) indicates an acceptance of the unconscious self. Such an acceptance leads the quester to the last stage of his journey and to his final trial with the destructive anima. In the bits of the lost novel included in the poem, Merrill does not elaborate upon this stage of the quest, which would have involved a confrontation between Leo and Joanna, but simply asserts that the destructive anima was to be routed before the novel's completion. In the final sections of "The Book of Ephraim," we are given a full account of every stage of the quest, including JM's defeat of the destructive anima that is transformed into a poetic muse.

Once the quest cycle is complete, it repeats itself, beginning with another traumatic fall. We have already seen an example of the ending and restarting of the quest cycle with JM's acceptance of Miranda, symbolizing the acceptance of the destructive anima and the completion of the quest cycle, which leads directly to JM's sin of pride by which he attempts to engineer the birth of Ephraim's representative as proof of the spirit's existence. After JM's final victorious quest, which concludes in section X, the poet abandons the quest and concludes the poem, rather than allow the cycle to continue its endless repetitions.

The primary quest in "The Book of Ephraim" is JM's quest for the sublime, whom allows and enables his writing of this poem. The poem itself is the "damsel in distress" whom JM must rescue. Ephraim is the symbol of this poem. He represents the poem in potential. In order to succeed in his quest to write this poem, JM must devote himself fully and unequivocally to Ephraim. The first twenty-one sections of "The Book of Ephraim," A thru U, are concerned with JM's efforts to commit himself to his familiar spirit. These sections are analogous to the sections in Dante's *Divine Comedy* in which Virgil is instructing and guiding the poet. JM's relationship with Ephraim is not so much that of quester to guide, or of student to teacher, as of lover to beloved. Ephraim is figured most prominently in this poem as a fickle beloved and a jealous lover.

In "The Will," Ephraim plays the role of the upstart lover who will go to any lengths to separate his beloved (JM) from older attachments, particularly from his longtime lover and Ouija board companion, DJ. Ephraim admits that he has long sought to "possess" JM for himself:

> YR SPIRIT HAS BEEN CAUGHT REDHANDED
> IT IS HIS OCCUPATIONAL FAIBLESSE
> TO ENTER & POSSESS REPEAT POSSESS
> L OBJECT AIME Who, me? WELL I HAD PLANNED IT
>
> WITHOUT SO MANY DAVIDS TO COMBAT
> MY GIANT DESIGNS UPON YR ART MON CHER
> SHRINK TO THIS TOPSYTURVY WILLOWWARE
> IGLOO WALTZING WITH THE ALPHABET (SP 275)

Since DJ cannot be gotten out of the way, he has to be used to produce Ephraim's representative, "The Book of Ephraim." The familiar spirit is ruthless in his implied dismissal of DJ, telling JM to "GIVE UP EVERYTHING EXCEPT THE GHOST" (SP 276).

The relationship between DJ and JM becomes increasingly strained as Ephraim grows in stature. The couple's estrangement grows as the poem progresses. In section K, JM says: "While DJ dreams, I retch all night," and later in Istanbul they turn up in opposing colors, "Blue DJ's, red JM's" (CL 37). In section G, JM says simply of Ephraim's strong hold on their lives: "We don't challenge him" (CL 22). But Ephraim challenges *them*, telling JM that the life he is living will be his last life on earth, whereas DJ has several more lives to go before graduating to the celestial hierarchy. DJ and JM protest that Ephraim is being insensitive to their relationship. Ephraim's response to this is significantly "unrecorded," and JM tries to brush the interchange away:

> The cloud passed
> More quickly than the shade it cast,
>
> Foreshadower of nothing, dearest heart,
> But the dim wish of lives to drift apart. (CL 25)

But the reader does not fully believe that the cloud has passed, for directly preceding this passage, the poet has written:

> We take long walks among the flying leaves
> And ponder turnings taken by our lives.
>
> Look at each other closely, as friends will
> On parting. This is not farewell,
>
> Not now. Yet something in the sad
> End-of-season light remains unsaid. (CL 23–24)

We are uncertain if the farewell the poet refers to is the impending goodbye on parting or the final farewell at the end of a relationship. The falling leaves seem to imply a death of feeling, if not of the relationship itself. These leaves turn up again in section Q in a quotation from Issa: "The wind gives me / fallen leaves enough / to make a fire" (CL 60). Fire is both purifying and destructive, implying both a beginning and an end. The ambiguity of the symbol is typical of this poem, which is about both the incarnation and the withdrawal of a god (CL 3). One god's or lover's death prepares the way for the birth of another.

Ephraim is the reigning deity of this poem; it is his "Book." But his authority is constantly being challenged by various "minor deities" from JM's "real" life, all of whom must be defeated before JM can fully devote himself to his familiar spirit. At the beginning of section G, both Maya, the poet's friend, and Maisie, his kitten, arrive upon the poem's stage. Ephraim perceives both as threats. Maya is introduced to Ephraim through the Ouija board and finds him "too much the courtier living for pleasure" (CL 23). Ephraim's response to Maya's criticism discloses the jealous and possessive side of his nature: "LETS HOPE THE LIVED FOR PLEASURE WILL NOT BE / ALL MINE WHEN YR WHITE WITCH SETS EYES ON ME" (CL 23). Maisie, the cat, is an unlikely threat. Nevertheless her "Calico self-possession" is "promising to outpoise by ounces / Ephraim as the household heavyweight" (CL 23). In the poem's narrative, Maisie is soon defeated. She is described as being no longer a kitten but "the half mad old virgin Henry James / Might have made of her, and this James had":

The side of me that deeply took her side
Was now a wall. Turning her face to it
She read the blankness there, and died. (CL 51)

Ephraim's "COUP DE GRACE" (CL 66) in his fight to win possession of JM is his "defeat" of the novel that JM "loses" and decides not to rewrite. Merrill figures the lost novel (including the character of his alter ego Sergei) as a flower that Ephraim "nipped in the bud" (CL 66):

Pallid root-threads. A blue sky inverted
In waterglass. The Greek geranium
Snapped off last week unthinkingly lives on.
Forgets that, short of never to be born,
Best is an early, painless death.
. . . .
It seems to tolerate me, turn to me
For—ah, not strength, or even company,
But cooly, as who have no more to lose
Welcome a messenger from the gods.
Live on—is that the message? Dear Sergei,
It is what we do against all odds. (CL 68)

This geranium parallels the "avocado in a glass of water" in "The Broken Home" that the poet nurtures and destroys. His loss complete, Sergei returns to his maker, the poet of "Ephraim." The poem comes to seem the poet's one consolation for his many losses. If the poet is to lose both his novel and his companion DJ, then he may find consolation in the poem, where he as god may insure that "nothing's lost" (SP 284).

This quotation is taken from Merrill's lyric "Lost in Translation," which concludes with the poet's Proustian reassurance that art and memory can provide consolation for life's losses:

But nothing's lost. Or else: all is translation
And every bit of us is lost in it
(Or found—I wander through the ruin of S
Now and then, wondering at the peacefulness)
And in that loss a self-effacing tree,
Color of context, imperceptibly
Rustling with its angel, turns the waste
To shade and fiber, milk and memory. (SP 284)

The ruin of S refers to a failed love affair between JM and a Greek man named Strato. But we may also think of it from the point of view of *The Book of Ephraim* as being the "ruin of Sergei," the one wholly admirable character in the lost novel. Sergei is modeled on an acquaintance whom the poet has used before as material, fashioning him into a character in the ballad "The Summer People" (SP 167). That poem ends with the character's suicide. He is born again in *The Book of Ephraim*—"old self in a new form" (CL 68), proof that art can save what has been lost and saved and lost again, if at a price.

The tree above is "self-effacing," which points to the fact that the artist must sacrifice himself to his work, *become* the "color of context," absorb the "waste" of his life by turning it into art, wrestling with his angel or muse in order to force from him a blessing, "milk and memory." The creator of Sergei and of "Lost in Translation" is willing to believe that the unending struggle to save the self in art is worth the price that art exacts from life. Although the "scribe" is never "immune" (SP 303) and must take responsibility for his use of life for art, he is not responsible for the situation by which we are all forced into being users by the greatest user of all, which is time itself.

Addressing the flower that will soon wither, which stands for the abandoned Sergei of the lost novel, the poet considers his human weakness in the face of mortality, which forces him to use the world, including his own creations, as a shield from the absolutes of time and death:

> Tell me, tell me, as I turn to you,
> What every moment does, has done, will do—
> Questions one simply cannot face in person.
> Freshening its water, I feel faint
> Waves of recognition, my red flower
> Not yet in the dread phrase cut-and-dried. (CL 68)

The relationship between life and art is never "cut-and-dried." The creator is both used and user, rebel and god. His memories and creations, flung in the face of mortality, having themselves become immortalized *through* him, may turn upon him, serving as a reminder of the self that has been lost. Life progresses while the poet digresses, to the point at which he is forced to "cut" his losses and undo his own creations:

> Too violent,
> I once thought, that foreshortening in Proust—
> A world abruptly old, whitehaired, a reader
> Looking up in puzzlement to fathom
> Whether ten years or forty have gone by.
> Young, I mistook it for an unconvincing
> Trick of the teller. It was truth instead
> Babbling through his own astonishment. (CL 70–1)

A writer of Proust's or Merrill's strength can assimilate the truth of time lost into the work by which he is attempting to save it. Merrill saves what is already lost by allowing his novel to inhabit a space in its successor, "The Book of Ephraim." He is thus able to save the novel even as he abandons it. JM is likewise striving to save his relationship with DJ. If in reality the relationship is allowed to wither and die, it will nevertheless live on in the poem, as in memory. Poet and lover alike strive to make use of time's "waste" that "stops at nothing" (CL 71).

Creations that enable the creator to define and know the self in time become a stricture that the creator must throw off in order to free the self imprisoned in it. This is one theme of Richard Wagner's *Ring* cycle, and, although Wotan, unlike Brünnhilde, is not present in Merrill's poem, his unseen presence is felt—as in *Götterdämmerung*—in the poet's concern with the culpability and sadness of the creator who must destroy his creation to free the self invested and imprisoned in it. Wotan says in *Die Walküre*: "In the ruins of my own world / I would end my endless sadness" (253). Once a creator has invested in a creation to such an extent that he can no longer determine where the self begins and ends, he must destroy or abandon the creation to regain the self as a knowable entity, distinct from its environment.

When Merrill writes in *Ephraim* of his relationship with Strato, his Greek lover and a subject of several poems, he is considering the risk the author and lover runs when he aggressively invests himself in an unreliable exterior paramour. Ephraim facetiously accounts for Strato's questionable devotion by explaining that he is an "UNSEASONED SOUL" who is "IN HIS FIRST MANS LIFE," whereupon JM asks, "was he something else before?" (CL 50). Receiving no straight answer from Ephraim, the poet embarks upon his own examination of Strato's character.

> I recall virtues—Strato's qualities
> All are virtues back in '64.
> Humor that breaks into an easy lope
> Of evasion my two poor legs cannot hope
> To keep up with. Devotion absolute
> Moments on end, till some besetting itch
> Galvanizes him, or a stray bitch.
>
> (However seldom in my line to feel,
> I most love those for whom the world is real.)
> Shine of light green eyes, enthusiasm
> Panting and warm across the kindly chasm.
> Also, when I claim a right not written
> Into our bond, that bristling snap of fear
> Recalling which I now—and don't forget

> How often, Ephraim, one has played *your* pet—
> Take back my question. What he was is clear. (CL 51)

Strato is the poet's subject, his lover, and his pet. The individual who devotes himself fully to another has given over the right to feel to this beloved, whose attention alone can make the world seem real. The lover's "occupational weakness," like Ephraim's in "The Will," is the felt necessity to possess the beloved, to live vicariously through another. If the beloved is unavailable, the lover feels lost.

Poet and lover are both users whose aggression paradoxically makes them dependent upon another. Merrill is not content simply to castigate the user for being aggressive and unfeeling. Rather he shows how the user is punished by feeling itself. Part of the sensation of being in love is experiencing this silent transition of the beloved from pet to master. JM and DJ originally adopt Ephraim as their pet, whose "most fragmentary message" is "Twice as entertaining, twice as wise / As either of its mediums" (CL 7). In the beginning, Ephraim remains "sweetness itself" (CL 15). But he has a penchant for black humor that DJ and JM "trusted not one bit. / Must *everything* be witty? AH MY DEARS / I AM NOT LAUGHING I WILL SIMPLY NOT SHED TEARS" (CL 17). His unwillingness to shed tears shows a lack of empathy and a calculating nature—shades of the master he is to become.

Like every beloved, Ephraim is both deserving and undeserving of JM's devotion. He is a protective guide and a possessive user. At times, the poet views Ephraim's aggression from a wryly amused distance.

> Ephraim, who enjoys this flying trip
> Round the world more than we do, sees us next
> At the tailor's in Kowloon:
> MY DEARS I AM BEST SUITED WHEN U STRIP (CL 36)

Psychologically the user "possesses" his object by projecting his libido into it. The greater the object's effacement, the more opportunity the user has for successfully manipulating the object to his own end. That JM has become psychologically self-effacing is made clear earlier in the poem when he learns of his father's death and reacts with "16FOLD LACK OF EMOTION" (CL 36). This emotional vacuum provides Ephraim with ample opportunity as the user. DJ and JM know they are being used but view the situation from an ironic, metaphorical distance: "From the Osaka puppets we are learning / What *to be moved* means" (CL 36).

Looked at from another point of view, we can see Ephraim's growth into the "household heavyweight" (CL 23) as having been prompted by the growing estrangement between JM and DJ. Their estrangement is reflected in their environment, which is decaying:

> The whole house needs repairs. Neither can bring
> Himself to say so. Hardly lingering,
> We've reached the point, where the tired Sound just washes
> Up to, then avoids our feet. One wishes—
> I mean we've got this ton of magazines
> Which *someone* might persuade the girl who cleans
> To throw out. (CL 41)

As in "The Will," the poet-narrator seems unwilling to take responsibility for his life. Caught in such paralysis of will, the lovers welcome Ephraim's possessiveness. Through him, they are able to refuse responsibility for their own actions:

> we fall
> Back on the greater coziness of being
> Seen by him, and by that very seeing
> Forgiven for the spectacles we've made
> Of everything, ourselves, the world, the mud
> Gullies skipped over, rut on trickling rut,
> All in the name of life. *Life?* Shh. En route. (CL 38)

By making themselves into "spectacles" for Ephraim's improved vision, they can avoid acknowledging "the mud gullies" of their decaying relationship. Such an abandonment of will to the unconscious (of which Ephraim is the representative) and the resulting identity crisis are necessary steps in the quester's journey for renewal. He must lose himself in order to find himself. He is "En route."

Before JM can experience renewal, he must devote himself fully to Ephraim, the symbol of the sublime revelation that will enable that renewal. Ephraim's aggressiveness in relation to his disciple, JM, makes a full commitment difficult. JM's reluctance is made evident in his abandonment of Ephraim. The trip to his analyst symbolizes JM's lack of faith in his familiar spirit. Immediately preceding this section in the poem, we are given a scene in which DJ is put under hypnosis by JM in order to "see" Ephraim. Once under hypnosis, DJ is "possessed" by Ephraim, assuming a "voice not his, less near, / Deeper than his, now limpid, now unclear":

> It had grown cool, impersonal. It led
> Me [JM] to a deep black couch, and stroked my face
> The blood had drained from. Caught up in his strong
> Flow of compulsion, mine was to resist,
> The more thrilled through, the less I went along,
> A river stone, blind, clenched against whatever
> Was happening that once. (CL 27)

Ephraim uses DJ in this scene, which parallels the bedroom scene between Leo and Ellen in the lost novel. In DJ's description of the seduction scene, which he writes down the next morning, it was not himself but an "unemasculated Blake nude" in the room trying to seduce JM:

> *As he stroked J's face & throat*
> *I felt a stab of the old possessiveness.*
> *Souls can't feel at E's level. He somehow was*
> *using me, my senses, to touch JM who*
> *this morning swears it was my hand stroking him.* (CL 27)

Ephraim's inability to feel parallels JM's admitted weakness, which draws him to try to "possess" Strato "for whom the world is real." In this scene, Ephraim is trying to possess DJ and JM. JM's strength as a user in his own right seems to protect him from Ephraim's advances, as DJ wryly notes when describing JM's reaction to the stroking hand: "*Typical of J to keep, throughout, staring / off somewhere else*" (CL 27). DJ is in greater danger because of his "oldfashioned / Trust in nature human and divine" (CL 26). He finally resists Ephraim's advances: [DJ speaking] "*Now Ephraim tried to lead me / to the mirror and* I *held back*" (CL 27).

Later JM comes to see his unwillingness to put himself into Ephraim's hands as a failure of belief. Overcoming his skepticism, he devotes himself fully to his familiar spirit at the conclusion to section U. He implicitly accepts Jung's notion that god is the unconscious, whose representative is Ephraim:

> Jung says—or if he doesn't, all but does—
> That God and the Unconscious are one. Hm.
> The lapse that tides us over, hither, yon;
> Tide that laps us home away from home. (CL 74)

The "lapses" described in "The Will," which culminates in the novel's loss and the poem's conception, appear from the point of view of the nearly completed poem to have been a fortunate fall. The psychological "lapse" turns into the "laps" of the ocean wave that brings the wandering hero home. From the privileged perspective of having reached the shore, JM can see how the journey "down" into the depths of self and the unconscious has been the way up, the way home, all along:

> Onstage, the sudden trap about to yawn—
> Darkness impenetrable, pit wherein

> Two grapplers lock, pale skin and copper skin.
> Impenetrable brilliance, topmost panes
> Catching the sunset, of a house gone black . . . (CL 74)

The impenetrable darkness of the "pit" transforms into the impenetrable brilliance of the "topmost panes." The "pains" it has taken for the blinded-by-darkness quester to climb out of the pit (the blackened living room at the beginning of "The Will") and up through the psyche's house to be blinded by the light of revelation have been recorded in the poem. JM has been transformed from the blinded Oedipus, made unseeing by the darkness he finds within himself, to the blinded Dante beholding Beatrice, symbol of sublime love and devotion.

As JM implicitly pledges his devotion to Ephraim, the spirit is transformed from the guide to the divine to the symbol of the divine. He is forced out of the mutable world by his newly recognized immutability. Ephraim has gone to join "the golden things that go / Without saying, the loves no longer called up / Or named" (CL 85). By his absence, Ephraim insures JM's presence.

> Ephraim, my dear, let's face it. If I fall
> From a high building, it's your name I'll call,
> OK? (CL 74)

That Ephraim insures JM's existence by representing his secret and individual self is made clear by a comparison of the passage above to a parallel passage in the early novel, *The Seraglio*. The autobiographical character is speaking:

> "I'm too conscious to be happy," he began. . . . "If I were to fall nobody would catch me. I have to keep dodging people in the street. They never look where they're going. They could walk right into me and knock me down. It's always *my* consciousness." . . .
>
> "I should like . . . to do something at cross purposes, something *against* my consciousness. I should like to feel, no matter what I thought I was up to, that the real meaning of my action was hidden from me." (159)

Merrill's autobiographical character, Francis, inhabits the psychologically self-destructive state in which we find JM at the beginning of the poem "The Will." In that poem, the speaker describes how he nearly "removes" his thumb in a carving "accident." His repression of unconscious desire is leading to dire consequences. In the novel, Francis' repression of desire is finally, brutally, overcome only after he fails to take his own life by cutting off his sexual organ. In this act, the desperate conscious self tries to rid itself once and for all of the unconscious and its ungovernable libido. Having survived this self-destructive act,

Francis enters a new life made full by the forced acceptance of previously unconscious desire. Francis' psychic wholeness results in his first love affair with a man and their taking up of the Ouija board together.

Years later the older poet is considering the loss of both of these companions—DJ, his lover, and the Ouija-board spirit, Ephraim. Their threatened loss is obliquely referred to by the poet's mentioning of Strato, JM's old lover, and by his reference to Kleo, his old servant in Greece.

> Now let me go downstairs to pack,
> Begin to close the home away from home—
> Upper story, lower, doublings, triplings,
> Someone not Strato helping with my bags,
> Someone not Kleo coming to dust and water
> Days from now. (CL 53)

Kleo also turns up in section O, where the poet writes:

> We won't see her name in writing till she retires.
> "Kleo" we still assume is the royal feline
> Who seduced Caesar, not the drab old muse
> Who did. Yet in the end it's *Clio* I compose
> A face to kiss, who clings to me in tears.
> What she has thought about us all God knows. (CL 53)

The goddess of love turns into the goddess of history. Our individual history of love is paid homage to in salty tears and in the wrenching *tears* with which we turn away from any failed relationship. These tears leave their marks, scars that we carry with us throughout life, representing both failure and success.

Throughout the poem the poet refers to these scars as "scratches on a mirror" which over time force a pattern on our lives, the "illusion of coherence" (CL 88). In this way, all devotions are finally assimilated into the "bigger picture" of our life:

> Set in our ways
> As in a garden's, glittered
> A whole small globe—our life, our life, our life:
> Rinsed with mercury
> Throughout to this bespattered
> Fruit of reflection (CL 41–42)

Remembering that Mercury is the alchemical god of transformation, the conduit—like Ephraim—between the mundane and the divine, we can see how the poet attributes to him our powers of "reflection." We would have no means of reflection and no matter to reflect upon if it were not for the "bespattered" flaws in our mind and memory that allow us to see a pattern in the mirror of consciousness. This pattern indicates a world beyond consciousness that represents a larger vision of the self. The mirror's "flaws," the sublime "spatters" of mercury, or the "scratches" on the surface of consciousness are the doorways through which our life passes in the sublime moment, moving from the mundane, "that craze / Of its own creation / Into another life" (CL 42), the life of revelation.

Throughout the poem the sublime moment of revelation is signaled by the conjunction of images of fire and water, symbolizing the coming together of opposites, the joining of the unconscious to the conscious, and the ideal to the real. At times, the poet uses a symbolic shorthand to signal the sublime moment, as when he describes Miranda's island: "Raw earth reds and sky blues" (CL 18). We may take "red" to stand for fire, as "blue" represents water. In other instances, the symbols are more elaborate, as when the poet describes the hypnosis session in which DJ hallucinates Ephraim into being:

> The room
> Grown dim, an undrawn curtain in the panes'
> Glass night tawnily maned, lit from below
> So that hair-wisps of brightness quickened slowly
> *the limbs & torso muscled by long folds of*
> *an unemasculated Blake nude. Who then*
> *actually was in the room, at arm's length,* (CL 27)

The darkened window (symbol of water) is "lit from below," illuminating the "hair-wisps of brightness" that are analogous to the spatters or scratches on the mirror. These stand for a world "beyond reflection." This idealized world of the unconscious is represented by the figure of Ephraim, whose hallucinated, materialized figure is the product of the sublime conjunction of water and fire.

The result of these moments of revelation, symbolized by the trials of fire and water, is the loss of the old, conscious self. The quester is renewed by the experience of the God within. In section V, JM walks through a "window fiery-mild" (CL 77), marking the beginning of the poet's final revelation. This trial by fire concludes with the poem's conclusion as the poet instructs himself: "put this light out / Fix a screen to the proscenium / Still flickering" (CL 92). Having fixed the "fire screen" in place, the quester is prepared to reenter the real world. He has been renewed by the purifying journeys behind the waterfall, the mirror, and the flickering proscenium. These are the trials by fire and water that symbolize the quester's reacquaintance with the elemental self, the divine child-self within each of us who remains an eternal virgin, immune to aggression, jealousy, envy, and remorse. The self won by the quester who successfully completes his trials is both old and new. It is a wiser but also innocent self. The quester's rediscovery of this self is tantamount to a moral regeneration.

The poet describes such a regeneration early in the poem when JM "re-lives" the death of a self from a previous incarnation. The "dead" self is Rufus Farmetton, a young South African boy who died in 1925, one year before JM's birth. JM experiences the death of Rufus Farmetton in reverse order, beginning with the moment the young boy dies and progressing to an earlier moment in which he gains an ambiguous but profound knowledge:

> I *know.*
> Eyes in the mirror—so I've woken—stare,
> Blue, stricken, through a shock of reddish hair
> —Can we stop now please? U DID WELL JM
> DEATHS ARE TRAUMATIC FEW REMEMBER THEM (CL 43)

The passage leaves us unsure as to what JM as Rufus Farmetton knows. But since it details the last days of the young boy's life, in which he finds proof of the "betrayal" of his closest friend by reading his unattended journal, we can assume that he has discovered something about the secret relation between the written life and the life that is lived. Devotion to one necessitates neglect of the other. The "eyes in the mirror," which have "woken" the beholder, are indication of such a self-revelation. This realization leads JM, through the reverse chronology of the scene, from death to rebirth. The scene ends at the moment preceding the revelation of betrayal that prefigures Rufus Farmetton's actual death. JM emerges from hypnosis a symbolically innocent self, having reached the moment before the Fall into the knowledge of good and evil ("I *know*"), which follows the awakening of self-consciousness, represented by the stricken "eyes in the mirror." This sublime moment of self-revelation is signaled by the conjoining of water and fire images, the "blue" eyes and "red" hair seen in the mirror.

In section Q, Merrill gives us another version of the conjunction of fire and water that leads to self-knowledge and a symbolic rebirth. The poet quotes from Peter Quennell's biography of Alexander Pope, in which the author describes Pope's "famous grotto." The description indicates that a visit to this grotto is symbolic of a trial by fire and water since "every surface sparkled shimmered or gleamed" and the sound of an underground spring "echoed through the cavern day and night . . . Pope intended . . . that the visitor, when at length he emerged, should feel that he had been reborn into a new existence" (CL 61). That Merrill stands for Pope and is leading his reader into such a "rebirth" through the trials by fire and water of his poem is supported by Ephraim's assertion that in one of JM's previous lives he had been an editor of Pope's works (CL 12).

After JM devotes himself fully to Ephraim in section U, he is faced with the awesome responsibility that such an acknowledgment implies. He has accepted that he alone is responsible for his own salvation or damnation. He finds little comfort in this knowledge.

> what vigilance will keep
> *Me* from one emblematic, imminent,
> Utterly harmless failure of recall.
> Let's face it: the Unconscious, after all . . . (CL 74)

The artist must be ever-vigilant as he struggles to save what *can* be saved from oblivion. One thinks of Proust working all night long in self-imposed exile. The utterly harmless failure of recall might be the missing piece to life's puzzle. We recall Merrill's most Proustian poem, "Lost in Translation," in which the missing puzzle piece takes years of experience to fit into place.

In section V, we find JM at the crossroads of his journey. He must decide whether to devote himself to explicating the revelations that his relationship with Ephraim have made available to him or whether to leave well enough alone and return to the creation of his lyrics of "love and loss." JM's position in V is analogous to Leo's position before the waterfall in the lost novel. To step behind the falls is to meet his "double" accuser and to declare independence from the "great mother" who has dogged him throughout his poetic quest.

Before meeting his double accuser, JM first has to step through the waterfall, symbolically accepting the implications of Ephraim's revelations. JM finds his symbolic waterfall, fittingly enough, in the canal city of Venice.

> Venise, pavane, nirvana, vice, wrote Proust
> Justly in his day. But in ours? The monumental
> "I" of stone—on top, an adolescent
> And his slain crocodile, both guano-white—
> Each visit stands for less. And from the crest of
> The Accademia Bridge the (is that thunder?)
> Palaces seem empty-lit display
> Rooms for glass companies. Hold still,
> Breathes the canal. But then *it* stirs,
> Ruining another batch of images. (CL 75)

Many battles are being fought at once in this passage. Section V is the closest Merrill comes in *Ephraim* to addressing the dilemma of the "post-modern." We hear echoes throughout of the great modernist lament, *The Waste Land*, not only in the poet's references to "thunder," "canals," and "bridges," as well as his use of Dante, and his cosmopolitan mixture of languages, but also in the general aura of displacement and disillusionment that he creates. From the viewpoint of the late-century poet, even the moderns seem fortunate. They were able to fashion great works of art out of their disbelief and disillusionment. But, in our day, Merrill implies, art itself is suspect. It is no longer immune from the hollowness and emptiness of the surrounding civilization. Neither is the "academy" immune. From the crest of *its* bridge, one sees only surfaces, "empty-lit display rooms."

Merrill seems to be concerned here with the distrust of and lack of interest in the "transcendent" world *behind* the glass or mirror. Transcendence is not possible without a "self" to transcend. This understanding too is under attack. The "monumental 'I' of stone," to which Merrill refers in section W as the "representable self," now "stands for less." The adolescent and his slain crocodile is a reference to section X with its reliance on Giorgione's *La Tempesta* and Wagner's *Ring*. Both are representations of the hero's quest through fire and water. In section V, the poet questions whether the "guano-white" contemporary self is worth saving.

The poet strives to rescue what is salvageable in a "batch of images," only to find them "ruined" by the very current of life that led to their creation: The canal says to hold still and then "*it* stirs." The poet implicitly questions whether it is possible to create a transcendent work of art in a world that distrusts the possibility and value of the effort itself:

> A Lido leaden. A whole heavenly city
> Sinking, titanic ego mussel-blue
> Abulge in gleaming nets of nerve, of pressures
> Unregistered by the barometer
> Stuck between Show and Showers. Whose once fabled
> Denizens, Santofior and Guggenheim
> (Historical garbage, in the Marxist phrase)
> Invisibly—to all but their valets
> Still through the dull red mazes caked with slime
> Bearing some scented drivel of undying
> Love and regret—are dying. And high time. (CL 75)

The "leaden" Lido contains a sly reference to the base material that the alchemist seeks to transform into a precious substance. (We will remember that Jung, Merrill's instructor in the use of alchemical metaphor, viewed the whole of alchemy as a metaphor for psychic individuation.) The poet is the alchemist who feels the "pressures" of trying to save the precious "heavenly city" before he himself sinks, like the *Titanic*, into a quotidian paralysis, "stuck between Show and Showers," between the normal routine and intermittent crises of human life. JM's experience with Ephraim has given him this brief opportunity to achieve a greater knowledge of self and world. Still, he is worried that this poem, in which he has striven as never before to bring life and art together in one "undying" homage to "love and regret," will end up on the historical garbage heap along with modernism itself, represented by the inclusion of Peggy Guggenheim, the famous patron of modern artists, and with his own "lost" novel, represented here by the "Marchesa Santofior," the "mythical" name of the the novel's heroine, Mrs. Smith. The crisis the poet is facing may be summed up in a question: "What if art cannot save life, at least not this life?"

The poet returns in section V to the dilemma of the childless artist faced with creating his own progeny out of his imagination. Those who invest themselves in children and family find security and self-knowledge in the child's reflecting mirror of the self:

> Some have come from admiring, others are hurrying
> To sit out the storm in the presence of Giorgione's
> *Tempesta*—on the surface nothing less
> Than earthly life in all its mystery:
> Man, woman, child; a place; shatterproof glass
> Inflicting on it a fleet blur of couples
> Many of whom, by now, have reproduced.
> Who is Giorgione really? Who is Proust? (CL 76)

The individual with a child can point to that child as living proof of his own existence and can place in the child—and its offspring, or "reproductions"—his hopes for immortality. But the childless artist can point only to his creation as proof of his existence. This makes him fully responsible for his own preservation. The questions "Who is Giorgione really? Who is Proust?" ask us to ponder whether a painting or book can truly preserve the self.

Few artists have succeeded in saving their lives through art as fully as Proust, who strove "Through superhuman counterpoint to work / The body's resurrection, sense by sense" (CL 76). For all of Proust's strengths—Ephraim calls him "A GREAT PROPHET THRONED ON HIGH"—he cannot help JM get his own "senses somehow purified back" (CL 57). Realizing this, the poet declares that he will no longer live in the inhibiting shadow of his predecessors but will succeed at his own creation, saving himself in the process, or will give up on art altogether and accept his "lost" condition:

> I've read Proust for the last time. Looked my fill
> At the *Tempesta*, timeless in its fashion
> As any grid-epitome of bipeds
> Beeped by a computer into Space. (CL 76)

Although the reader can participate vicariously in Proust's "resurrection," it is not his own life that has been saved in this marvelous book, nor his individual story that is told in the *Tempesta*, but the generic ("grid-epitome of bipeds") story of "earthly life." The individual creative artist is alone in the position to save his life through art.

The poet acknowledges that the effort to save a life requires more of a sacrifice to art than he has been willing to make in crafting his lyrics of "love and loss," which he decides to abandon:

> No further need henceforth of this
> Receipt (gloom coupleted with artifice)
> For holding still, for being held still. No—
> Besides, I fly tomorrow to New York—
> Never again. Pictures in little pieces
> Torn from me, where lightning strikes the set— (CL 76)

We have examined the "gloom coupleted with artifice" in Merrill's early work, typified by the death of the metaphor at the end of a poem. Such conclusions as "Dust of my dust, when will it all be plain?" (SP 217) display the gloomy and witty artifice with which the poet faces a death that is not a transcendence but a dissolution. The void is glimpsed every time the poet is faced with crisis, when "lightning strikes the set" in a blinding moment—as of a photographer's flash—of emotion and artistic inspiration, leaving behind the picture, or poem, as residue of a crisis lived through, but also leaving the darkened "set," the poet-self, unenlightened.

In this turning point of his quest, the poet declares that he will prompt revelation-through-crisis and no longer wait for it to find him:

> Now give me the alerted vacuum
> Of that black gold-earringed baby all in white
> (Maya, Maya, your Félicité?)
> Her father focuses on. There. Come.
> One more prompt negative. (CL 76)

JM is seeking the "felicity" Maya found in her dream, described in section M, in which she finds that her black gown "turns to white" and "her jet to diamonds." She becomes her own negative, "a not yet printed self" (CL 44). In the felicitous world that Maya's dreaming self discovers, "black holes," which are present throughout the poem as metaphors of irretrievable loss, turn into stars, symbols of the eternal. The "black" baby is dressed "all in white," symbolizing the "positive" transformation of the "prompt negative." The "gold" earrings are another positive symbol, representing the alchemist's successful effort at purifying and transforming the black, "leaden" substance with which he began.

Like the photographer and the alchemist, the poet is seeking "transformation." He wants to translate his Dantean mid-life crisis into his greatest success and most enduring achievement. Like Proust, he would transform the black holes of loss, "the alerted vacuum," and the bitter disappointments of life—"prompt negatives"—into a work of art ensuring this life's immortality. He would "Transform, in time, time's damage; / To less than a black plume, time's grief" (SP 3).

In the conclusion of section V, Merrill attempts to document this transformation from loss to redemption, from the human to the divine—a transformation that by its very nature defies representation. The poet's effort at describing this transmutation is a technical and narrative highpoint of the poem:

> Gust of sustaining timbers' creosote
> Pungency the abrupt drench releases—
> Cold hissing white—the old man of the Sea
> Who, clung to now, must truthfully reply— (CL 76)

The scene described is of a "tempest." Remembering that the Latin *tempestas* means time as well as storm, we will understand that the poet-quester is represented in this scene as riding out the storm of life on a sea of time, seeking to "transform, in time, time's damage."

The sought-after transformation is further attested to by the alchemical symbolism of the passage. The "sustaining timbers" not only hold the ship together in the storm but also fuel the alchemical fire. The "abrupt drench" may be thought of as the base metal's plunge into the crucible to be purified, releasing "cold hissing white—the old man of the Sea." The appearance of the white substance represents the trapping of the elusive spirit Mercurius in the alchemical "vessel," just as it represents, in the "tempest" reading of the passage, the ship or "vessel" becoming itself caught in the raging storm. The transformation of the inner self is simultaneously a transformation of the outer world.

In his study of alchemical transformation, Jung quoted from the crucial *Rosarium* text: "The spirit Mercurius descends in his heavenly form . . . to purify the blackness" (PT 111–12). This spirit exists in potentiality in the base matter itself but requires "release" before he can assume his heavenly form. This freeing process requires both patience and skill on the part of the alchemist, who must work to purify the base material without burning it up. (We remember that the first spirit whom JM and DJ clumsily try to contact on the Ouija board is being "burned" alive in a warehouse fire.) The elusive Mercurius is "ever about to flee" before the crucial transformation of the base metal (the unpurified, "unwritten" self) into the precious substance or work of art is complete (PT 108). The poet-quester must "cling" to this Protean spirit, the muse of transformation, pursuing him "from one bride chamber to the next" (PT 132). The bridal image is fitting. The sublime that the quester seeks is a marriage of inner and outer realities. We see evidence of the spirit-bride's coy evasions in Merrill's elaborate method of containment, the dense layering of symbol and meaning throughout this difficult passage, and in his rapid transitions from one layer to another.

It is fitting that this passage dramatically displaying the poet's power should follow the passage in which he has declared his artistic independence. Announcing that he has "read Proust for the last time," he symbolically destroys the book that has most sustained him through life's storm. In doing this, he follows the cryptic advice of the *Rosarium* writer, who instructs the alchemical quester to "rend the books lest your hearts be rent asunder" (Jung, PT 112). Jung argued that the rending of the books represents the abjuring of intellectualism, what Gaston Bachelard has called "psychologism," the "thinking" that impairs "feeling" (PT 117). The ego-quester seeking individuation is in danger of believing that, having understood the process, he has completed it. To avoid this mistake, he forcibly separates himself from the intellect, or what Blake called "reason," which hinders "desire." In artistic terms, this forcible separation from the intellect is played out as the rebellion against one's precursors, whose completed quests in book form must be imaginatively destroyed in order to make psychic space for the quest at hand.

The poet's willingness symbolically to enter the tempest and to cling to the old man of the sea indicates that he is no longer a disciple of others but is ready to be tried alone before the absolute. The image of the poet clinging to his muse reminds us of Jacob wrestling with his angel, whom he would not release until being given a blessing. The poet of *The Book of Ephraim* seeks the blessing of self-knowledge, and also the poem that this newly won assurance will enable and inspire.

Symbolically, the poet seeks to create a doorway for himself into the sublime. The conclusion of the passage in V depicts the making of this doorway, figured as the making of glass, which will turn into a "window" to be walked through—as the poet has previously "entered" the waterfall and mirror—into the world of essence, beyond reflection and appearance.

> Bellying shirt, sheer windbag wrung to high
> Relief, to needle-keen transparency—
> Air and water blown glass-hard—their blind
> Man's buff with unsurrendering gooseflesh
>
> Streamlined from conception—crack! boom! flash!—
> Glaze soaking inward as it came to mind
> How anybody's monster breathing flames
> Vitrified in metamorphosis
>
> To monstrance clouded then like a blown fuse
> If not a reliquary for St. James'
> Vision of life: how Venice, her least stone
> Pure menace at the start, at length became
>
> A window fiery-mild, whose walked-through frame
> Everything else at sunset, hinged upon— (CL 77)

This passage begins with the image of the blowing wind, a Biblical symbol for the appearance of the Holy Ghost and also a romantic symbol of inspiration. The task that the creative artist sets for himself is to contain this spirit, to give shape to the imagination by force of will. The poet strives to "harness" the spirit of creation with a "bellying shirt," the poem itself, figured here as a ship's sail, or as the molten glass that is being blown into and turned and shaped.

The "crack! boom! flash!" of the second stanza represents the aggression against the natural order necessary for creation in this mutable world. The "monster breathing flames" is the furnace of time itself, which prompts and enables all human endeavor. This passage also describes the final steps in the making of the symbolic glass vessel ("glaze soaking inward") in which our past lives are preserved as memories in the mind, like holy objects in a "monstrance" or "reliquary."

Acts of aggression give way to acts of atonement in the time-bound world. This is the determined world in which the non-questers who do not, in Ephraim's phrase, "WISH TO THINK" (CL 60), spend their lives, revolving between the poles of aggression and remorse, past and present, present and past. Out of time, in the sublime moment figured by the rare quester's passing through the "window fiery-mild," grace and menace become realities between which the individual must choose and upon which "everything else" hinges. This choice is available only to the quester "who, thinking, spends / His inmost dividends / To grow at any cost" (LS 74).

We can get a better sense of the crucial nature of this choice by looking at the way in which other modern poets have presented it to the reader. Wallace Stevens wrote in "The Well Dressed Man with a Beard":

> After the final no there comes a yes
> And on that yes the future world depends.
> . . . .
> If the rejected things, the things denied,
> Slid over the western cataract, yet one,
> One only, one thing that was firm,
> . . . .
>   would be
> Enough (PEM 190)

In this lovely poem, the whole of the quest for the sublime is encapsulated in the choice between "yes" and "no." Devotion is the key in Stevens' mind, as in Merrill's, to the successful completion of the quest in which necessity becomes choice. To arrive at this choice, finding "one thing remaining, infallible," worthy of devotion, is to be able to say "yes" unconditionally.

In *The Sea and the Mirror,* W. H. Auden figured the first step toward the sublime as the step through the mirror (of the dramatic stage) to the space behind the proscenium. He wrote that both mirror and proscenium are "feebly figurative signs" that represent the "essential emphatic gulf" between our quotidian existence and the "Wholly Other Life" of the sublime (CP 444). Those who make it to this place, this "Life," are given the choice between "yes" and "no." In this poem, Caliban represents Necessity, the denial of the transcendent that is represented by the spirit Ariel. Caliban explains the choice between himself and Ariel to those few who make it behind the proscenium of life's appearance:

> you have now all come together in the larger colder emptier room on this side of the mirror which *does* force your eyes to recognize and reckon with the two of us, your ears to detect the irreconcilable difference between my reiterated affirmation of what your furnished circumstances categorically are, and His [Ariel's]

successive propositions as to everything else which they conditionally might be. You have, as I say, taken your first step. (CP 435–36)

This is the step that JM takes when he walks through the "fiery-mild" window into watery Venice. In section W, JM is confronted with the choice between "yes" and "no" when he meets his nephew Wendell, who represents Caliban's negating view of life. Ariel is represented in the passage by Venice itself and by the artistic splendors—Wagner's *Ring* and Stravinsky's *The Rake's Progress*—associated with its glorious past.

The accusing Caliban self becomes recognizable every time the ego-quester is willing to venture into the unconscious. In section H, when DJ is hypnotized, Ephraim "materializes." In section L, when JM undergoes self-hypnosis with Ephraim's instructions, he experiences a previous incarnation. In both cases, the real self is not lost but doubled, as is Leo when he ventures behind the falls in the lost novel. The poem's most enduring double is the spirit Ephraim, whose name means "double fruitfulness" (*The Oxford Dictionary of English Christian Names*). In each case, the appearance of the double offers both opportunity and risk. The quester must integrate the double without becoming subsumed within it. In section W, Wendell poses the greatest and final challenge to the ego-quester. The defeat and integration into the self of all that he stands for is the turning point that allows JM to complete his journey and begin the poem's creation.

In terms of the poet's quest for psychic individuation, the encounter with Wendell represents the dangers of solipsism and narcissism. Whenever the ego ventures into the unconscious, it faces the danger of becoming obsessed with the combination of great beauty and repulsiveness that the double figure represents. Wendell is beautiful: His hair is "merman blond," and he has "sparkling blue" eyes. JM's reaction to Wendell's youth and beauty is not strictly that of an uncle to a nephew, as he coyly informs us. But JM finds Wendell's view of human nature and achievement repulsive. Like JM, Wendell is an artist, a painter, but unlike Merrill, he is not for the "happy ending." Rather, "pain, panic and old age / Afflict his subjects horribly":

They lie
On pillows, peering out as from a cage,

Feeble or angry, long tooth, beady eye.
Some few are young, but he has picked ill-knit,
Mean-mouthed, distrustful ones. When I ask why,

Why with a rendering so exquisite—?

> "I guess that's sort of how I see mankind,"
> Says Wendell, "Doomed, sick, selfish, dumb as shit." (CL 79–80)

Wendell is a Tadzio figure to JM's Aschenbach. He represents the amoral innocence and harsh judgments of youth. To the older, more experienced JM, his cynicism must seem unearned. Nevertheless, his allure is real. JM faces the danger of failing to take Wendell seriously on an intellectual level, as he refused at first to take Ephraim seriously, while idealizing Wendell's youthful beauty. In the worst case scenario, JM would "take on" Wendell as an "object" for the projecting self, as Aschenbach does with Tadzio. In such a relationship, there is no recognition between individuals. The pair relate to one another as subject to object. This is the relationship we have explored in our discussion of JM and Strato. In "Caliban to the Audience," Auden argued that the self that would create its own idealized subject desires the amoral "freedom to transcend *any* condition . . . without *any* . . . obligation" (CP 440). The self that insists on creating its idol/ideal will eventually find that this ungiving, amoral mirror has usurped the self's integrity. In Blakean terms, the created ideal is not a contrary, a "You," who leads to growth and self-awareness, but a negation, an "it," which is unaware and unmoving. The "narcissistic beautiful boy" ideal is a literary convention depicting the sterile and solipsistic nature of the relationship between a manipulative, self-protective lover and an ignorant, unfeeling beloved.

Throughout "Ephraim," we have seen examples of an individual's encountering the mirrored, doubled self and treating it as an ideal, as in JM's relationship to Sergei, Ephraim, and Strato, as well as in Leo's relationship to Eros. In each situation, idolatry turns into enslavement, after which the lover is forced to destroy this double self and shatter his symbolic mirror, in order to free himself from its control. By section W, the mythical progress of the poem has quickened to such a degree that the idealized double is encountered, recognized, and destroyed in straight order.

Wendell is a blood relation of the poet. He is thus closer to the "real" JM than are previous doubles. This indicates to us that the quester is coming to the end of his journey. He is approaching the objective world that he abandoned when beginning his poem and quest. In section X, we are given further proof that we are approaching the objective world when the poet identifies his mother as the archetypal feminine. As the poem nears conclusion, art and reality draw ever nearer. The mythical quest-romance of the Ouija board merges with the poet's family drama.

Faced with Wendell's cynical opinion of human nature and achievement, JM is instinctively eager to maintain "the illusion / That whatever had been, had been right" (CL 63).

> "The self was once," I put in, "a great, great
> Glory." And he: "Oh sure. But is it still?
>
> The representable self, at any rate,
> Ran screaming from the Post-Impressionist
> Catastrophe . . ." (CL 80)

The problem of representation has been Merrill's concern throughout *Ephraim* and is intrinsically tied to the issue of the self's integrity. The "I" without a "self" cannot create great art because it lacks self-knowledge. *The Book of Ephraim* is concerned with JM's search for enlightenment. Like Proust, JM will have found his vocation and subject matter when he discovers the self as a knowable and representable entity.

The issue of representation is given even greater weight in this passage when we discover that Merrill has no nephew named "Wendell." He has chosen, in this one instance, to include a major "fictional" character in the poem and not label him as such, intentionally blurring the line between life and art that he has so carefully traced throughout the rest of the poem. Merrill seems to prepare us for Wendell's entrance and implicitly defends his fictional creation, in section U, when he considers the loss of Ephraim:

> Shall I come lighter-hearted to that Spring-tide
> Knowing it must be fathomed without a guide?
> With no one, nothing along those lines—or these
> whose writing, if not justifies, so mirrors,
> So embodies up to now some guiding force,
> It can't simply be written off. In neither
> The world's poem nor the poem's world have I
> Learned to think for myself, much. The twinklings of
> Insight hurt or elude the naked eye (CL 85)

The poet is lost without his material, without someone or something to mirror and embody. With Ephraim as his mirror, JM feels that he is in collusion with "some guiding force." Without Ephraim, he is a "naked eye" unable to perceive itself. When JM loses touch with Ephraim, he loses the one mirror for which he has forsaken all others, especially his relationship with DJ and the fictional characters of the lost novel. He finds himself in the position of having to "create" a mirror self in order to fuel the poem's creation.

Wendell is JM's created mirror, his self-born accuser. The poet implicitly refutes Wendell's charge that the self is no longer a "great glory" by representing Wendell in technically brilliant *terza rima,* the stanza Dante used for his *Comedy.* Like Eliot in *The Waste Land,* Merrill seeks to refute charges against culture and self by the accomplishment of the poem in which the charges are being made. Writing in *terza rima,* the poet pays homage to and challenges his great precursor, implicitly demanding that his work be set alongside that of the past master.

JM destroys the solipsistic self represented by Wendell when he appeals to the ideal of devotion to another. He makes his appeal through references to two operas in each of which the heroine's devotion determines the final outcome of the drama. JM is leading Wendell through the streets of Venice when

a wrong turn
Discovers where the Master of the *Ring*
Once dwelt, the same who made Brünnhilde spurn

Heaven's own plea, ecstatically cling
To death-divining love, while the sky-folk
—Scene I, so help me, first heard Flagstad sing—

Touched by her tones' pure torch, go up in smoke.
And here is La Fenice where the *Rake*
Rose from the ashes of the High Baroque;

And here, the marble quai whence they would take
Largo by gondola Stravinsky, black
Drapery snagging sun-spokes in his wake,

Moons waning in the Muses' Almanac,
For burial past—see that far, bobbing light?
Wendell . . .? But we parted some time back (CL 81)

The narcissistic double departs when JM aligns himself with "death-divining love," devotion to another. In section Q, Merrill includes the quotation from *Götterdämmerung* referred to above in which Brünnhilde spurns heaven's plea. In the scene, Brünnhilde's sister has come to beg her to return the ring, the symbol of Siegfried's devotion, to its original owners, the Rhinemaidens. Unless Brünnhilde does so, her sister warns, their father Wotan and all of Valhalla will be destroyed. Brünnhilde responds:

Geh' hin zu der Götter heiligen Rath!
Von meinen Ringe raune ihnen zu:
Die Liebe liesse ich nie,

mir nähmen nie sie die Liebe,
stürzt' auch in Trümmern Walhall's strahlende Pracht!
(CL 62)
(Go back to the gods' holy council.
Tell them this about my ring:
I will never renounce love,
and they shall never wrest love from me,
though Valhalla's sublime splendour
Collapse in ruins!)

Brünnhilde is fulfilling Wotan's death-wish in her action, preparing the way for a new world. JM's renunciation of self-love in the form of Wendell is analogous to Brünnhilde's suicidal spurning of Valhalla's plea. A Biblical analogy can be made to Christ's refusal to be lured by Satan's worldly temptations in the desert, which prepares the way for the crucifixion. All are renunciations of the present world in favor of a world of pure potential. Without this renunciation, JM would have been like Narcissus at the pool, paralyzed by the impasse between subjective and objective experience.

This is the impasse that Tom Rakewell comes to in Stravinsky/Auden-Kallman's *The Rake's Progress* after giving his double self control over his will. As with JM and DJ in their attempt at "genetic engineering" through Ephraim's good offices, Tom is tricked by his double, Shadow, into believing that the real and the ideal can be imaginatively merged through force of will.

I wished but once, I knew
That surely my wish would come true,
That I
Had but to speak at last
And Fate would smile when Fortune cast
The die.
I knew, I knew! (56)

By the end of the opera, Tom discovers that he has sold his soul and forfeited his free will to Shadow, who comes to take his payment. Tom is "saved" at the last moment by the thought of his devoted "Anne Truelove" to whom he gives himself in despair: "Love, first and last, assume eternal reign; / Renew my life, O Queen of Hearts, again!" (168). By his devotion to "Truelove," Tom destroys the narcissistic double, but the ordeal has made him insane, and he dies soon after.

JM cannot die; he must survive to write the poem. But he is shaken by his trial with the narcissistic double, Wendell:

our struck acquaintance lit no drowned

Niche in the blue, blood-warm Palladian

> Sculpture maze we'd surfaced from, which goes
> Evolving Likeness back to the first man,
>
> Forth to betided lineaments one knows
> Or once did. I lose touch with the sublime. (CL 82)

The poet seems to be lamenting the fact that moments of insight are moments only. With the passing of time and nearing the conclusion of the poem, he seems to be questioning what he has learned from his ordeal and voicing doubts about the wisdom he has attained. The poet-quester seems to be losing faith in the worthiness of his quest.

He is saved from his doubts by the poem itself, which is living proof of "the life lived . . . of the love spent" (SP 59). At the conclusion of W, the poet offers a direct response to the doubts voiced at the beginning of section V concerning the worthiness of artistic endeavor:

> I lose touch with the sublime.
> Yet in these sunset years hardly propose
>
> Mending my ways, breaking myself of rhyme
> To speak to multitudes and make it matter.
> Late here could mean, moreover, In Good Time
>
> Elsewhere; for near turns far, and former latter
> —Syntax reversing her binoculars—
> Now early light sweeps under a pink scatter
>
> Rug of cloud the solemn, diehard stars. (CL 82)

In this passage, we witness the emergence of a poetic persona, the poet as prophet, rarely seen in Merrill's work before *The Changing Light* and glimpsed only momentarily in *The Book of Ephraim.* This persona will grow to huge dimensions in the second and third books of the trilogy, usurping the place of Merrill's previous persona as poet of love and loss. *The Book of Ephraim* marks the height of Merrill's achievement as the lyric poet of love and loss. The poet has exhausted his genre and must move on.

Having defeated his self-born accuser, the poet-quester comes face to face with his final opponent, the destructive anima, figured as the dragon of myth and the evil stepmother of fairy tales. In section X, we are given the most complete version of the defeat of the destructive anima in the poem. The poet strives to wed myth to reality by recognizing the people in objective reality who represent or have represented the feminine half of his bisexual psyche. He attempts to make his peace with these figures, accepting the feminine nature within himself.

JM begins his battle with the destructive anima by admitting that the most real symbol of the threatening feminine in his life is his mother. We are told as much with the poet's consideration of Giorgione's *La Tempesta*. The painting is based upon the myth of St. Theodore's killing of a dragon. According to legend, the dragon had abducted Theodore's mother and was holding her hostage. X-rays have shown that the painting's original scene was painted over. In an article upon which Merrill relied for his description of the painting, Nancy Thompson de Grummond contends that Giorgione's original scene had depicted Theodore's mother before her abduction, with the dragon looming in the foreground. The final composition depicts the scene after Theodore's slaying of the dragon and the rescue of his mother. In this revised representation, Theodore is standing in the spot where his mother had been in the painting's first version, and his mother is standing, with a child "who needs explaining," in the dragon's former position. The dragon itself "has been relegated / To a motif above a distant portal" (CL 83) in the painting's final form.

Theodore takes his mother's place and his mother displaces the dragon, which is itself "relegated to a motif." Recognizing that the destructive anima is often figured as a dragon in myth, we might interpret the painting's transformation using Jung's system of archetypal symbols. The mother in the original painting is the feminine half of Theodore's psyche. Like Miranda in Merrill's version of *The Tempest*, she is the symbol of the potentially harmonious relationship within the self between the feminine unconscious and the masculine conscious halves of the bisexual psyche. The dragon of the original painting represents the "projected" version of the feminine unconscious that has not been accepted by the psyche as a part of the self and has therefore become "destructive."

Theodore takes his mother's place in the painting's revision, symbolizing that he has defeated the dragon of the unconscious, thereby liberating the feminine half of the psyche, as represented by his young mother in the original painting. Having won the battle with the destructive anima, he can rest "at ease"—but not totally at ease. The fact that his mother is standing in the dragon's former position and that the dragon still exists as a "motif" indicates that she is still a threat. She may yet regress into her dragon state. Her holding of the child "who needs explaining" may be taken as proof that she *will* regress into that state. The child is best interpreted as Theodore himself, prior to his having undergone the quest for psychic adulthood.

The painting represents a circular myth, from innocence, with the child in its mother's arms; to guilt, represented by the "original" painting in which the dragon threatens the mother; to repentance, with Theodore's undepicted slaying of the dragon; and back to innocence, the painting in its present form, where the presence of the "mute hermit," recalling Sergei of the lost novel (CL 67), would seem to imply that all sexual and archetypal tensions have been resolved. In its "dual" form, the painting represents a complete myth cycle, a "snake that swallows its own tail" (CL 83).

The struggle between the feminine unconscious and masculine conscious is depicted in the painting as the struggle between mother and son. That Theodore is engaged in a struggle with his mother is attested to by the fact that "Grown up, he will / Destroy a temple to the Magna Mater, / And his remains still cause electric storms / In our day" (CL 83). The "friction" between mother and son is so strong that the grown-up hero is compelled to destroy the temple devoted to the child's figure of the "great mother." In his description of the painting's transformation, Merrill is calling forth the same situation as in the fourth sonnet of "The Broken Home." The hero is forced to face the mother-dragon who threatens to overwhelm him with her love. If he slays the dragon, he will have earned his right to love, not simply to be the object of another's love. Love is not love until it becomes subject to choice. The masculine search for a willed love begins with the male child's psychic separation from the protective figure of the mother. But the dragon of dependence is never finally slain, as the appetites of the unconscious are never totally sated. Psychologically, Theodore's task is never complete. He must slay dragon after dragon. He is the symbol of an archetypal struggle that will outlive him. His "remains still cause electric storms in our day."

Beneath these layers of myth and metaphor lies Merrill's relationship with his mother. Referring to the *Tempesta's* mother/son motif, he writes:

> All of which lights up, as scholarship
> Now and then does, a matter hitherto
> Overpainted—the absence from these pages
> Of my own mother. Because of course she's here,
> Throughout, the breath drawn after every line,
> Essential to its making as to mine;
> Here no less in Maya's prodigality
> Than in Joanna's fuming—or is *she*

> The last gasp of my dragon? I think so;
> My mother gave up cigarettes years ago
> (And has been, letters tell, conspicuously
> Alive and kicking in a neighbor's pool
> All autumn, while singsong voices, taped, unreel,
> Dictating underwater calisthenics). (CL 83–84)

JM's willingness to recognize the "hitherto overpainted" matter of his mother's absence allows him to admit of her integral role in the poem and in the self, "essential to its making as to mine." He can see that his vicious portrayal of Joanna and his sometimes equivocal portrait of his friend, Maya, are both reactions against the anima, against his own feminine nature, as best represented by his mother. All of these feminine figures combine to such a degree that when the poet asks, "is *she* / The last gasp of my dragon? I think so," we are uncertain who *she* is. It seems most likely that he is referring to his mother, since in the next line he informs us that she is no longer "smoking." But we know that the Oedipal fire is never finally extinguished.

Merrill's self-rebuttal here is excessively coy. When he tells us that his mother is performing underwater calisthenics to "singsong" voices, only those familiar with Wagner's *Ring* will get the point. His mother is performing the role of the Rhinemaidens who are present at the beginning and conclusion of Wagner's great work. Their cavorting presence at both ends of the tetralogy is a symbol of the cyclical myth to which Wagner gave new life and on which Merrill is working his own changes. It is the archetypal story of "the incarnation and withdrawal of / A god" (CL 3), which Merrill calls his "theme" in the introduction to "Ephraim." With the poet's oblique reference to the *Ring,* we are assured that this is *not* the last gasp of his dragon. Life is cyclical, like the creation-destruction myths themselves, "Siegfried and his worm / Slain among rhinestones, the great wordsmith Joyce / Forging a snake that swallows its own tail . . . / Ringed round by fire or water, their women sleep" (CL 83). Art is called upon to rescue the self from flames or flood time and time again.

By the conclusion of *Ephraim,* the poet has pushed the lyric as far as it will go in his hands in search of the sublime. He has traced the "naked current" of creation as it runs back and forth between inner and outer realities, repeatedly finding the self and losing it again. His exhaustion with the unending task of trying to contain the uncontainable is evident in his last reference to the lost novel, which concludes with the characters' exhausted surrender to necessity:

The novel would have ended with surveyors
Sighting and measuring upstream from the falls.
A dam projected. The pueblo elders
Have given in, not that they had much choice.
Next year there'll be no waterfall, no stream
Running through Matt and Lucy's land. They're lucky,
A Department man explains. Communities
Three or four miles West will be submerged.
On the bright side, it means a power station,
Light all through the valley. "Light," he repeats,
Since the old husband shakes his head. And she:
"Oh . . . light!"—falsely effusive, not to belittle
Any redress so royal, so . . . Words fail her.
What did I once think those two would feel? (CL 84)

The novel would have ended fittingly with the damming up of the stream of creation. Life turns into light at its own expense. We remember the little poem "Log," which ended with the poet's helpless rhetorical question as the log burned to ashes, "What could be made of you but light, and this?" (SP 189). Life fuels light as experience is transformed into art. The dam stops all forward motion, arresting experience to produce the light of art.

Ephraim begins with the novel's loss, its "damming up," and feeds itself on the novel's sublimated energy. The poem thus lives at the novel's expense. As the poem progresses, the novel is gradually consumed. The poet himself becomes more and more effaced. By the conclusion of "Ephraim," the quester has regained a "self," but one that has been "used up" in the poem's making. He concludes section Y:

And here was I, or what was left of me.
Feared and rejoiced in, chafed against, held cheap,
A strangeness that was us, and was not, had
All the same allowed for its description,
And so brought at least me these spells of odd,
Self-effacing balance. Better to stop
While we still can. Already I take up
Less emotional space that a snowdrop.
My father in his last illness complained
Of the effect of medication on
His real self—today Bluebeard, tomorrow
Babbitt. Young chameleon, I used to
Ask how on earth one got sufficiently
Imbued with otherness. And now I see. (CL 89)

The poet sees by the light of the poem that has been fueled by his life. He sees a picture of desolation and desertion, the self hollowed out by art. The "young chameleon" referred to here is the "pint-size amphibian" (SP 274) of the poem "The Will" that serves as preface to

"Ephraim." In that poem, we remember, the poet begins the quest by assuming the symbolic guise of the chameleon, symbolically accepting responsibility for actions hitherto ascribed to fate. Throughout *Ephraim*, this chameleon self has metamorphosed repeatedly, taking on the guise of master and servant, dragon-slayer and dragon, user and used, until the point where the self becomes so self-effacing that it is barely recognizable *as* a self: "And here was I, or what was left of me."

At the conclusion of the poem, the poet is preparing to release the "old man of the Sea" (CL 76), damming up the Protean stream of creation that has led to self-knowledge at life's expense. This conclusion is not a victory but a surrender, at best a stalemate. The poet has learned the hard truth of Ephraim's statement, "NOTHING LIVE IS MOTIONLESS HERE" (CL 60). There is no stopping the stars that JM observes at the end of section W from turning into the "Heaven . . . all peppered with black holes" (CL 85) at the conclusion of section X. The poet is giving up not because he has discovered the sublime that he sought but because he has discovered the limitations of human nature: "Higher than this I do not, dare not climb" (CL 71).

A sense of the ridiculousness of the human condition permeates the conclusion of "Ephraim." The poet seems to be laughing through his tears.

> Zero hour. Waiting yet again
> For someone to fix the furnace. Zero week
> Of the year's end. Bed that keeps restlessly
> Making itself anew from lamé drifts.
> Mercury dropping. (CL 90)

We get a feeling of exhausted anticipation from this passage, of waiting for someone or something that will, in any case, be too late to make a difference. The signs are ripe for an arrival. The "zero" hour and week seem to mark the end of a countdown, and, with the reference to the "dropping" of the alchemical holy spirit, "Mercury," we expect *something* to happen. But nothing does. This world is paralyzed by the quotidian. The glories of the imagination seem beside the point. The bed can make itself; it does not need human assistance. The furnace *does* need fixing, but the paralyzed JM is helpless before it and must wait for divine assistance.

The furnace in this passage and elsewhere in the poem is, like Blake's furnace, a dual symbol that stands for both our fallen condition and the imagination's efforts to reach beyond this condition. The broken furnace in *Ephraim* symbolizes the failure of the imagination to break out of the quotidian. It represents the poet's loss of faith in the power of the imagination to combat necessity. When the furnace is functioning, the poet is able to see the disparity between the necessary and the imagined, and he can seek to bring the two together. When the furnace is broken, however, no distinction is made between what is and what can or should be.

Imaginative symbols that mark the opening into the sublime elsewhere in the poem cease to work in Section Z. The "walked-through" window that plays such a crucial role at the conclusion of section V remains a barrier in Z:

> Windows and sliding doors are wadded shut.
> A blind raised here and there, what walls us in
> Trembles with dim slides, transparencies
> Of our least motion foisted on a thereby
> Realer—falser?—night. Whichever term
> Adds its note of tension and relief. (CL 90)

The window is a mirror creating "dim slides," but the quester does not take advantage of this opening into the sublime. He is paralyzed by doubts and unbelief. Reality and falsehood appear to him to be interchangeable and convenient categories that serve only to add "tension and relief" to a homogeneous existence.

The quest pattern continues in section Z, but the quester is no longer a willing participant. Both the double figure, which was last dispensed with in section W, and the "Great Mother," which the poet came to terms with in section X, reappear in section Z in their earlier threatening forms. The poet-quester's former victory over these figures is rendered incomplete by their reappearance, indicating to the reader that this conclusion will not conclude the quest sequence but simply restart the struggle detailed in the preceding pages.

The quest of Z is a parody of the successful quest of sections V, W, and X, in which JM encounters and momentarily defeats his doubts. Taken together, these three sections serve as the mythopoeic climax of the poem. By contrast, the poet-quester of Z is exhausted and ironic, firmly untranscendent. The space he claims for himself is not the vast, mythic expanse of Venice but the family hearth, and he is not even certain of his mastery over this smallest of dominions:

> Night before last, returning from a dinner,
> We found my bedroom ransacked, lights on, loud
> Tick of alarm, the mirror off its hook
> Looking daggers at the ceiling fixture.
> A burglar here in the Enchanted Village—
> Unheard of! Not that he took anything.
> . . . .

The threat remains though of there still being
A presence in our midst, unknown, unseen
Unscrupulous to take what he can get. (CL 90–1)

The conjunction of the mirror and the light overhead (water and fire images) marks the entrance to the sublime quest and is followed by the appearance of the double figure. But since the poem is nearly finished, and since poet and reader are preparing to step back into reality, the double figure is no more than a shadow, "unknown, unseen," a doubt in the mind instead of the full-blown self-accuser of an Ephraim or a Wendell. His threat to the poet is real though:

Next morning in my study—stranger yet—
I found a dusty carton out of place.
Had it been rummaged through? What could he fancy
Lay buried among these—oh my dear,
Letters scrawled by my own hand unable
To keep pace with the tempest in the cup—
These old love-letters from the other world.
We've set them down at last beside the fire.
Are they for burning, now that the affair
Has ended? (Has it ended?) (CL 91)

By disturbing the "dusty carton," the unseen double plays his archetypal role of leading the quester to scrutinize the self, implicitly ordering the quester to look into the buried box. But the doubting poet who asks in Y "How sensible had *we* been / To dig up this material of ours?" (CL 87) is unwilling to undergo further scrutiny. He considers burning the Ouija-board manuscripts, the symbols of the "other world," that the double represents. Like Francis in *The Seraglio*, the quester of Z is tempted to silence all criticism from and contact with the other world in one brutal, self-destructive act.

Any day
It's them or the piano, says DJ.
Who'll ever read them over? Take this one.
Limp, chill, it shivers in the glow, as when
The tenor having braved orchestral fog
First sees Brünnhilde sleeping like a log.
Laid on the fire, it would hesitate,
Trying to think, to feel—then the elate
Burst of satori, plucking final sense
Boldly from inconclusive evidence.
And that (unless it floated, spangled ash,
Outward, upward, one lone carp aflash
Languorously through its habitat
For crumbs that once upon a . . .) would be that. (CL 91)

Wagner's cyclical myth is the primary reference point of this passage. The devotion of Brünnhilde and Siegfried for one another, born in the moment when the hero, "having braved orchestral fog," first lays eyes on the heroine, is the fuel that feeds the fire of *Götterdämmerung*. Their love propels the old world to destruction in order to make way for a new creation. The poet's simile comparing Brünnhilde's sleeping figure to a "log" reminds us once again of the poem "Log" and its assertion that necessity is the ruling influence of this mutable world. The poem's conclusion, "What could be made of you but light, and this?" (SP 189), seems proof of the individual's helplessness before necessity.

The contradiction between necessity and devotion, which makes all things possible, is analogous to Stevens' seemingly contradictory statements, cited by Merrill in section S, that God and the imagination are one and that the imagination presses back against the "pressures of reality" (CL 66). In section Z, as in S, Merrill attempts no resolution of the contradictions. But the poet's tone in Z is much darker than in S. Whereas in S the reference to Stevens' contrary assertions leads to an acceptance of Ephraim's guiding power and the rejection of the lost novel, all of which implies "progression" in JM's poetic quest, the emphasis in Z is on the repetitive nature of the quest. The proposed burning of the manuscripts is implicitly compared to the phoenix's immolation, leaving behind the "spangled ash" as source of its assured rebirth. In this passage, the ash metamorphoses into a "carp aflash" searching for crumbs. This brings us back to the beginning of the poem when the questers' first communication with the other world through the Ouija board is compared to the catching of a fish:

> Was anybody there? As when a pike
> Strikes, and the line singing writes in lakeflesh
> Highstrung runes, and reel spins and mind reels
> YES a new and urgent power YES
> Seized the cup. (CL 6)

The poet's coy reference with the "carp aflash" to the beginning of the poem, in which the fish is caught and the "affair" with the other world is begun, seems to indicate that the burning of the manuscripts would be a false ending. There is no "final sense" to be gotten from their "inconclusive evidence." They are their own sense, proof and pudding alike.

The rest of the poem gives us further indication of the poet's willingness to let the poem "live" and also of his exhaustion with the task of creation in his quest for the sublime:

So, do we burn the—Wait the phone is ringing:
Bad connection; babble of distant talk;
No getting through. We must improve the line
In every sense, for life. Again at nine
Sharp above the village clock, *ring-ring*.
It's Bob the furnace man. He's on his way.
Will find, if not an easy-to-repair
Short circuit, the failure long foreseen
As total, of our period machine. (CL 91)

As at the conclusion of section W, the poet calls into question the worthiness and usefulness of the poetic task, this "period machine." By comparing the poet's creativity to a machine, he parodies the effort he has made throughout the poem. This effort has had the effect of exiling the poet from life in the service of art.

In order to "improve the line . . . for life," he finds it necessary at the end of the poem to punish his creation through parody. Writing "Again at nine, / Sharp above the village clock," he makes reference to the highest stage in Ephraim's (and Dante's) world of the sublime. But the word "again" implies that the ninth level is reached automatically and repeatedly. The quester is compared to the hands on the clock, which go round automatically like the cogs of a machine. The clock here may remind us of Eliot's clock in *The Waste Land*, which keeps watch over the ghostly figures flowing over London Bridge "With a dead sound on the final stroke of nine" (CPP 39). As in Eliot's poem, "nine" is sad proof of the failure of the imagination to win a victory against necessity.

The quester's willingness to leave the "fixing" of the poetic machine to fate, whose representative here is comically referred to not as an angel of mercy, prophecy, or deliverance, but simply as "Bob," is proof of his helpless state and of his ambivalence in relation to the poem that he has created out of the revelations he has received. Proust's "Law," which Merrill defines in "Days of 1971," is proven once again: "Only when time has slain desire / Is his wish granted to a smiling ghost / Neither harmed nor warmed, now, by the fire" (SP 235). JM considers his nearly completed poem with an indifference so profound as to be hostility, impishly considering whether he should burn his manuscripts in order to preserve the piano's space.

The manuscripts' subsequent reprieve seems more the result of exhaustion on the part of their author and proposed destroyer than of the recognition of any worth or wisdom they may hold.

Let's be downstairs, leave all this, put the light out.
Fix a screen to the proscenium

> Still flickering. Let that carton be. Too much
> Already, here below, has met its match.
> Yet nothing's gone, or nothing we recall.
> And look, the stars have wound in filigree
> The ancient, ageless woman of the world.
> She's seen us. She is not particular—
> Everyone gets her injured, musical
> "Why do you no longer come to me?"
> To which there's no reply. For here we are. (CL 92)

We are thus returned to the darkened downstairs room that the poet occupies at the beginning of "The Will," the unlit lower chamber of the first stanza of "The Broken Home." The poet has come full circle, reattaining that state of blissful ignorance—"nothing's gone, or nothing we recall"—that allows us to live our lives. This is a state of acquiescence in which the ego-quester, having forged a shaky alliance with his unconscious brother, allows that brother to go his own way, renouncing the self's authority over itself, which was proclaimed at the end of section U with the statement: "God and the Unconscious are one" (CL 74). As the poet-quester prepares to reenter life at the end of section Z, the unconscious is allowed to become, once again, unconscious: "Let that carton be."

Despite the poet's ambivalence, however, his quest has not been futile. He *has* changed, as is proved by his reception of the "ancient, ageless woman of the world." At the beginning of his quest, in "The Will," this feminine figure was labeled "The bad fairy Carabosse" (SP 277). Through the quest of "Ephraim," she has been transformed into the muse and mother of section Z. Her transformation is the crucial element in the transformation of Merrill's poetry from the quest-romance of *The Book of Ephraim* to the comedy of *Mirabell's Books of Number*. In this second book of the trilogy, the poet's dead friend, Maria Mitsotáki, assumes the mantle of the gentle and protective woman of the world. She is primarily responsible for guiding DJ and JM through the "divine comedy" of *Mirabell* and *Scripts*. Her own transformation near the end of *Scripts* into a campy masculine figure marks the poet's final and most crucial defeat of the feminine. This transformation, from the fertile feminine into the sterile masculine of the drag queen, is tantamount to the poet's destruction of his muse, and it leads to the poem's final and most convincing conclusion.

The conclusion of *Ephraim*, beautiful as it is, is not a convincing end to the poet's quest. He has once again coupleted gloom with artifice, producing "one more prompt negative" (CL 76). But the stage is set for the next act. The poet has learned the futility of confronting the natural order directly. Henceforth, he will employ the comic mode to undermine the natural order indirectly, allowing that there is "NO ACCIDENT" (CL 179), while creating a private, saving mythology in an effort to rival his great predecessors—Dante, Blake, and Yeats.

4

Solving this Riddle of Appearances: *Mirabell's Books of Number*

> And when that day dawns, or sunset reddens, how joyous we shall all be! Facts will be regarded as discreditable, Truth will be found mourning over her fetters, and Romance, with her temper of wonder, will return to the land. The very aspect of the world will change to our startled eyes.
>
> —Oscar Wilde

By the end of *The Book of Ephraim* the poet's quest for the romantic sublime has deteriorated into a vision of the absurd. The poet's journey into the unconscious in search of self-knowledge exposes him to the crass libidinal engines that drive the machine of man's animal nature. Elsewhere, Merrill refers to this libidinal center as a "greedy, erotic little orc" (CL 433) and a "faceless will" (SP 36). This is the same unconscious, natural will to which the poet surrenders himself in the poem, "The Will," which serves as an informal preface to *Ephraim*. The poet-quester's journey through *The Book of Ephraim* is led by this natural will, personified in the spirit Ephraim. JM's quest exposes him to previously unknown heights and depths of the self, but it also proves to him that a human being cannot live at either extreme and that continual vacillation between the two will result in the absurdist vision of life that we receive at the end of the poem.

Mirabell's Books of Number serves as an antidote to this vision of the absurd. The spirits who rule in this book warn against too heavy a reliance on natural will, for nature is synonymous with "CHAOS" (CL 113). *Ephraim* is an emotivist poem in which the poet strives to portray the joy and pain given and received from loves won and lost, devotions and betrayals. In *Ephraim*, the poet is seeking to reveal the lineaments of his personality by contrasting the pleasure he has received with the guilt he has incurred by devoting himself to one lover over another, to art over life, and to himself over all else. In order to gauge his pleasure and pain accurately, the poet needs to feel strongly. He is repeatedly frustrated by his limited ability to understand and represent these feelings: "What I think I feel now, by its own nature / Remains beyond my power to say outright" (CL 84). As the poem progresses, the quester senses his capacity for feeling diminishing: "Better to stop / While we still can. Already I take up / Less emotional space than a snowdrop" (CL 89).

The spirits of *Mirabell* warn that they too have lost their feelings, which "WENT UP IN FLAME" (CL 113) as a result of their continuing worship of nature, which they call Chaos. They implicitly warn JM that too much concern with a revelation of the hidden nature of the self will result in the loss of "personality," the ability to feel real in a real world. By relating their painful history of having fallen into a state of impersonality, the spirits are seeking to warn the poet about the dangers of becoming fixated on the hidden and selfish motives that fuel the libidinal furnace. They urge JM to accept the knowledge of self that he has won through the quest of *Ephraim*. It is a mistake, they argue, to believe that "KNOWLEDGE IS EVIL" (CL 115), even if it is knowledge of evil itself, the amoral desire at the base of all action. Having accepted the knowledge of evil, JM is urged to resist, using every means at his disposal (CL 202). The spirits tell the poet: "THE DEVIL HAS BEEN DRIVEN FROM US INTO MAN WE NOW / MUST DRIVE IT OUT OF HIM OUR TOOLS ARE MIND WORDS REASON LIGHT" (CL 114). Using these mind-based tools, the spirits instruct JM to "RAISE A SONG TO OUR REAL ORDER MYND AND NATURE WEDDED" (CL 113).

The poet of *Ephraim* perceives an essential division between mind and nature, the ideal and the real, what we think of ourselves and what we really are. In that poem, the war between these factions is presented as a schism in the singular self: "The figure in the mirror stealing looks / At length replied, although its lips were sealed: 'Contrary to appearances, you and I / . . . Have not seen eye to eye. We represent / Isms diametrically opposed'" (CL 69). The poet's growing awareness of this schism between appearance and reality leads him to the vision of the absurd. The poet of *Mirabell* is being urged to correct this double vision by creating a unity out of the apparent disunity of mind and nature.

The picture that the spirits paint at the beginning of *Mirabell* is of a universe out of joint because of the enmity between its ruling deities. As in *A Midsummer Night's Dream*—which might be seen in the background of this poem, as was *The Tempest* in *Ephraim*—every least part of the natural order suffers because of the gods' estrangement. Matter itself is locked in combat with anti-matter. JM and DJ suffer as well. They are described as patients and convalescents. Their eventual release from the sickroom, "WITH A CLEAN BILL OF HEALTH" (CL 269), is dependent on their willingness to do their part in patching up the marriage of mind and nature. JM says, "I think we're meant / To save that marriage, be the kids who stay / Together for their parents' sake" (CL 229). DJ's responsibility is to serve as the "hand" at the Ouija board, while JM is instructed to create "POEMS OF SCIENCE" (CL 109).

In creating a poem of science wedding mind and nature, Merrill is attempting to create a vision of an ordered and benevolent universe by which he can bridge the chasm between the ideal and the real—the chasm that led to the vision of the absurd in *Ephraim*. Merrill's precursors in this endeavor to represent the whole self in an ordered universe are two of the great epic poets of Christianity, Dante and Blake. John Milton seems to have made little impression on Merrill, since he is mentioned rarely in the entire epic, and this in passing. By contrast, Dante and Blake are referred to throughout the trilogy as acknowledged models in the task of creating a poetic world that will bring into harmony the discordances of self and history. In accomplishing this task, all three poets seek the wedding of mind to nature. But the terms "mind" and "nature" mean very different things for each poet.

Merrill is typically "of two minds" about each term. Nature is represented as being "Mind's equal / . . . mother, sister, bride" (CL 229), the intuitive, instinctual half of the marriage that steps in when the rational mind perceives more reality than it can bear, proffering the "forgiving smother of her humus" (CL 232). But nature is also the source of man's ignorant and merciless libidinal drives that repeatedly direct him to "MATE PROPAGATE & DIE" (CL 229). Mind is both a loving spouse who "Held by [nature's] beauty and inventiveness / Comes to love—INDEED AD NAUSEUM" (CL 231) his eternally youthful bride and the one protection that humans have against Nature's "clinging vine" (CL 232), which would return us as quickly as possible to Mother Earth. Through its creations of culture and civilization, the mind allows man to aspire to the immortality that the spirits claim is every human's wish (CL 314).

The spirits and questers of *Mirabell*, having experienced firsthand the powerful and destructive draw of chaos (the spirits through their loss of paradise and the questers through their vision of the absurd as described in *Ephraim*), are inherently anti-nature. In both *Ephraim* and *Scripts*, the natural, unconscious self is given primacy. But in this purgatorial volume, the ruling spirit Mirabell repeatedly praises the power of mind and reason at the expense of nature and instinct. He refers scornfully to our human bodies as "THE SLAPDASH STRUCTURES ERECTED BY NATURE TO HOUSE U" and claims that "NATURE WAS NEVER OF THE 1ST INTELLIGENCE" (CL 220). JM takes issue with Mirabell's scorn for nature in a "starstruck hymn to Mother N" (CL 235), in which he recognizes that natural will, for better or worse, fuels the machine of man and that a mind that conceives of itself as being separable from nature is self-deceiving. This hymn near the end of *Mirabell* prepares the way for the more positive view of nature we receive in *Scripts*.

For the poet of *Mirabell*, nature is an untrustworthy if necessary and at times generous mother. Mirabell argues that mind is required to chasten and chastise his spouse. In *Mirabell*, as in *The Magic Flute*, which is cited as a parallel (CL 248), the masculine principles of reason and rule are given primacy over the feminine principles of intuition and desire. But the poet acknowledges that such an ordering is inherently "unnatural" and is based on the mind's resistance to human nature.

In both Dante and Blake (as in *Ephraim* and *Scripts*), the figures are reversed. In the *Purgatorio*, Dante gives primacy to the self that obeys "amore, o naturale" (17. 92–93), natural love, which Blake calls "desire." When Blake writes, "He who desires but acts not, breeds pestilence" (151), he is warning of the dangers of disobeying this intuitive self and of falling prey to "restraining reason," the pride of mind. Dante's equivalent term to Blake's reason is "amore, o d'animo" (17. 93), mental or spiritual love, which, unlike natural love, is prone to error. Dante's accomplishment in his *Comedy* was partially enabled by the world in which he lived, to which Auden in *Mirabell* refers as being both "GULLIBLE & HEAVENLY" (CL 147). Dante believed in the existence of a "First Good" (17. 97) that could be revealed by allowing the "natural" intuitive self to guide one, step by step, heavenward. Speaking for our skeptical modern world, Auden implies that a belief in natural will as heaven-centered and benevolent is the wish-fulfilling belief of a gullible mind. After Freud, is it possible to believe in a divine *and* a natural will? Auden, speaking for Merrill, seems to say no.

"DANTE'S STRENGTH" derived from his world's "FIERCE CREDULITY," which allowed him to see "DREAM, FACT & EXPERIENCE" as "ONE" (CL 132–33). Dante's quest for enlightenment was understood by his world to be real as well as metaphorical. Beatrice was believed to be both the representative of heavenly love *and* a Florentine girl, as Christ was understood to be both God and man.

In such a believing and highly ordered world, the necessary hierarchy of abstractions in an epic poem made sense. As another character in *Mirabell* comments, "Everything in Dante knew its place" (CL 256).

By Blake's time, such a comprehensive and coherent world view was no longer possible. Speaking to Auden in *Scripts*, JM says, "Dante saw / The Rose in fullest bloom. Blake saw it sick. / You and Maria, who have seen the bleak / Unpetalled knob, must wonder: will it last / Till spring? Is it still rooted in the Sun?" (CL 363). Merrill's concern about the "health" of the rose was foreshadowed by Blake, who feared that his world had lost sight of the "First Good." Blake warned that the increasing belief in the comprehensibility of empirical knowledge was crowding out the space that Dante's world had reserved as primary for the instinctive—or, as he would put it, the "desiring" self. Blake's reaction to the scientific positivism of his day took the form of an attack on desire-inhibiting reason, and on empirical science in particular. He perceived that a society that places its faith in the empirical self will have little use or tolerance for the spiritual and poetic self made manifest through intuition and imagination. Through the creation of his elaborate poetic universe, Blake implicitly asserted that we *can* see eternity in a grain of sand, can wed mind to nature, if we allow spiritual desire to take its natural course, revealing the divinity inherent in matter.

Like Blake and Dante before him, Merrill asserts that the imagination has final authority over the rational mind because it is the proof and repository of man's divine nature. Mirabell claims that man's "IMAGINATIVE POWER" (CL 251) separates him from the beast, his evolutionary brother. Whereas the beast "BLITHELY FORESOOK THE TEAT FOR THE WATER HOLE," the human "APECHILD FIRST / HAD TO IMAGINE THE THIRSTQUENCHING VIRTUE OF WATER / . . . MAN'S 1ST STEPS WERE TAKEN IN HIS MIND" (CL 251). Mirabell refers to this imaginative power as God B's "MAIN MAGIC" (CL 251), the connecting link between the animal, man, and his divine creator.

By assuring JM that evolutionary man is nevertheless divine, Mirabell prepares the way for JM's creation of a poem of science that can bridge the gap between nature and mind by creating a vision of an ordered and comprehensive universe in which fable and fact are one. Merrill's poem is in direct response to Blake's condemnation of the self-limiting science of the Newtonian universe. Blake was forced to deny the scientific facts of his day in order to be true to what he intuited as the real nature of the universe. Merrill asserts that modern, relativity-based science is—in at least one fundamental and crucial sense—opposed to the empirical, positivist science against which Blake contended. Whereas the empiricists viewed phenomena as primary and unassailable, the modern scientist places phenomena in a secondary position to noumena. Gaston Bachelard, one of Merrill's cited influences and a major theorist of modern scientific philosophy, has argued that this difference in method between premodern and modern science indicates a basic change in our beliefs concerning the nature of reality:

> The relation between the phenomena and the noumena of science is no longer to be seen as some remote and rather indolent dialectics; it is, instead, an alternating movement which always tends toward the effective realization of the noumenon. . . . Science calls a world into being, not through some magic force, immanent in reality, but rather through a rational force, immanent in the mind. Whereas reason was, in the early days of science, formed in the image of the world, now, in modern science, the aim of mental activity is to construct a world in the image of reason. (NES 54)

Modern science's placement of noumena in a privileged position in relation to phenomena leads to an understanding of mind as being more than rational and of reason as being more than man's logical reaction to the phenomena he perceives.

When the spirit Mirabell instructs JM to "RENOVATE THE HOUSE OF MAN" by wedding mind and nature, he offers him an *improved* tool of "pure reason" with which to complete his task:

> WE HAVE PULLD DOWN THE SUPERANNUATED CHURCH
> & RAISED AN ALTAR TO THE NEW HOUSE GODLET: PURE REASON
> NOT IN THE VOLTAIREAN SENSE BASED ON KNOWLEDGE MERELY
> BUT REASON RUN THRU THE FIRES OF MAN'S CLONED SOUL A NEW
> ENERGY, A NEW THERMOSTAT WILL HEAT & LIGHT MAN'S HOUSE. (CL 239)

"Man's cloned soul" is an inclusive term for Merrill. It sets man apart from the beasts and connects him to divinity; the term includes both the imagination and the intuitive gifts of the unconscious. "Pure reason" for Merrill is both rational and intuitive, the merging of Voltairean reason and Blakean desire. To accept the notion of pure reason is to understand that there can be no clear demarcation between the rational, perceiving mind and the creative imagination. Perception is always, in some measure, apperception.

Language, the purely human element, is the medium through which these two halves of the knowing self are merged. Noumena and phenomena, mind and matter, come together in our use of words, as

Merrill asserts when he writes of the impossibility of avoiding the sentimental fallacy:

> This window overlooks a sick elm tree
> . . . .
> Putting it into words
> Means also that it puts words into me:
> *Shooting ringing ramify root green*
> Have overtones not wholly for the birds,
> And I am nothing's mortal enemy
> Surrendered, by the white page, to the scene. (CL 172)

The alternative to language is the blank page of nothingness. The scene is drained of meaning when mind offers no resistance to matter. Man's single weapon for resisting the blank void of chaos, for turning nothing into something, is language and its divine power of translation, metaphor. Mirabell instructs JM and DJ:

> NOW METAPHOR IS THE RITUAL OF THIS NEW REASON
> & OF WHAT RITES? THE RITES OF LANGUAGE
> . . . .
> THE REVEALD MONOTHEISM OF TODAY IS LANGUAGE (CL 239)

JM is instructed to use his poetic language in prophetic fashion to save the marriage between mind and nature. By persuading his readers of the divinity of language, he is to combat the dangers of self-destruction in a godless age, an age without a First Good. The spirits tell JM that, without a belief in an absolute as a final end to which all human endeavor strives, meaning itself becomes absurd.

The spirits' materialist symbol for the absolute is the single atom, the basis of all material life. The spirits admit that the atom is a metaphor, a "CALLING CARD" from divinity, which Merrill has picked up in the annals of post quantum-physics science. But they insist that all metaphor and all myth are based in reality. "IT IS REAL ALL IS REAL THE UNREAL I KNOW NOTHING OF" (CL 174). This poem argues that, if we dig deep enough into myth, we inevitably find matter. Conversely, our understanding of the nature of matter is inherently mythical. Myth and matter, mind and nature, are wedded in an ongoing play of opposites:

> WE MADE PARABLE & MYTH IN HARD
> BIOLOGICAL TERMS ADAM & EVE ARE IMAGES
> FOR DEVELOPMENTS IN THE VERY NATURE OF MATTER
> A WORLD NEGATIVE & POSITIVE DWELLS IN THE ATOM
> EDEN A STAGE THE EXPULSION THE DRAMA (CL 115)

Mirabell's revelation that myth is matter, which modern science allows by placing noumena in primacy before phenomena and which Auden supports in this poem when he informs JM that "fact is . . . fable" (CL 263), prompts Merrill's effort in this poem to resurrect belief in poetry and drama, in language itself, as more than mere fictions that may be discarded with impunity by modern man. To deny the power of language is to deny the nature of matter and, ultimately, to deny life itself. Bachelard, whose poetics on the "material imagination" Merrill has adopted in *Mirabell*, quotes Honoré de Balzac's comment on Dante, who, "Bible in hand, after spiritualizing matter and materializing the spirit, acknowledged the possibility of passing, through faith, from one sphere to another" (AD 53). Merrill is attempting to follow Dante, but, having no Bible to rely upon, he has turned to modern science, the one system that most educated people *do* believe in. According to Mirabell, the Bible has much in common with modern science:

THE BIBLE IS A CODE OF BLURRD
BUT ODDLY ACCURATE BIOHISTORICAL DATA.
NOT UNTIL THE APOSTOLIC TEXTS IS SOUL SURVIVAL
DEALT WITH, & THAT IN A COLLAPSING WORLD (CL 187)

Merrill's most important audience in this collapsing world is comprised of those few of more than common sense who have lost their religious belief (CL 246). To these, he offers language, the Word that is written in every atom (CL 243).

Man's disbelief in the power of the Word is equated by Mirabell with atomic man's blasphemous denial of the integrity of the single atom. The modern age of unbelief is coincident with the age in which the atom has been split; chaos, or anti-matter, has been released into the universe as the very source of evil (CL 114). In telling JM and DJ his mythological version of history, Mirabell explains how his race allowed this evil into the world in pre-human history through experiments with atomic fission, which they have equated ever since with the worship of chaos. The spirits tell JM: "THERE IS AN EVIL WE RELEASD WE DID NOT CREATE IT / CALL IT THE VOID CALL IT IN MAN A WILL TO NOTHINGNESS" (CL 120). They warn JM and DJ, "THE ATOM IT IS ADAM & LIFE & THE UNIVERSE / LEAVE IT TO ITSELF & LET IT BREATHE" (CL 118).

The spirits' admonition to the poet-questers, like so much else in this purgatorial volume, implies the necessity of accepting human limitation. In *Ephraim*, JM sought to stretch the boundaries of the knowable self and to reach beyond time. In *Mirabell*, he is learning to respect restraint. Early in the poem, when the cup that JM and DJ use as a pointer on the Ouija board is "swept clean off the Board" as an indication that "someone has overstepped," JM asks, "But will we never learn the limits?" (CL 107). This seems to prompt the elaborate instructions to follow.

Mirabell is a poem about the value and necessity of education. Its teachings are often in direct opposition to the questers' working assumptions in *Ephraim*. The centripetal quest for the motives of the secret self in the earlier volume is answered in *Mirabell* with a warning to respect the integrity of the central self, the mythical—and yet real—atom of human nature:

> THE ATOM, IS IT THE VERY GOD WE WORSHIP? IS IT
> ONLY AT GREAT RISK PURSUED? THE ATOM, IS IT MEANING?
> & IF SO WHAT BUT CHAOS LIES BEYOND IT? (CL 224)

Atomic physicists who would violate the atom are here equated with radical deconstructionists, who would frustrate meaning, and with the unbelieving "JOSTLERS FOR SELFREALIZATION" (CL 119), who, having short-sightedly abandoned their belief in an absolute, would embark on the self-destructive quest for self-realization. These atom/Adam-smashers have been lured by a "FALSE PARADISE" from which one may be saved only by clinging to "THE LIFE RAFT LANGUAGE" (CL 119).

The spirits have good reason to warn JM and DJ, having themselves fallen from just such a false paradise. Using chaos' divisive tool of atomic energy, they had built:

> A WORLD YOU CD NOT IMAGINE . . . IT WAS A
> SHINING CRUST OVER THE LAND & SEA
> . . . .
> A L L L I F E S O A R E D & THERE WAS NO DEATH
> AND THEN
> . . . .
> WE CHOSE
> TO MOVE ON INTO SPACE ABANDONING THE WORLD WE ROSE
> THE CRUST LIKE A VEIL SHREDDED FAR BEHIND US EXPOSING
> THE ALREADY ARID EARTH WE DESPISD IT & FLUNG BACK
> A LAST BOLT & THE UNIVERSE FELL IN ON US W E F E L L
> (CL 120)

Later in the poem, Mirabell tells the questers: "IN DESIGNING / OUR VAST ATOMICALLY POWERD WORLD WE FORGOT THE / VEGETABLE ADVERSARY" (CL 168). The history of Mirabell's race might be understood as a warning against the false sublime, a forced and narcissistic self-realization that is purchased at the expense of life itself. The false sublime is not the marriage of mind and nature but the banishment of nature in favor of a sterile, "mind-forged" ideal.

That Mirabell is referring to the divorce of mind from nature in his history of the fall is made clear by JM's questioning:

> Are we to take as metaphor your "crust
> World"—for, say, the brain's evolving cortex?
> . . . .
> These raw forces of mind called for the cortex
> To process them, is that it?—and the threat
> Of natural upheaval made you rise
> Where Nature couldn't. (CL 126)

In his hymn to Mother Nature, the poet asserts that man retreats to the sterile, ideal world of the mind in the belief that he might be "safe here, where security is vain" (CL 232). Mirabell's tale points up the vanity of this human wish to escape reality, which so often, in this age of therapy and analysis, takes the form of the potentially self-deceiving search for self-realization. Mirabell's assertion that the atom and indeed "ALL ENERGY SOURCES MUST BE KEPT COVERD" (CL 126) is a variation of Freud's seemingly anti-Freudian admonition to the questers in *Ephraim* that they respect the integrity of the self and refuse to give up the secret of their natures (CL 30).

As with so much else in this difficult poem, Mirabell's fall must be understood in several ways. In a material sense, Mirabell is warning against modern man's reliance on atomic energy and reminding us that our planet is endangered by our addiction to nuclear power and weaponry. In this material sense, modern man's position is unique in history. Psychologically, Mirabell is warning against the "split" between mind and nature with which the questers in *Ephraim* are so destructively obsessed. The spiritual danger that man faces has never changed; he is endangered by the one true evil in the world, the will to nothingness, which Mirabell cites as the source of both the narcissistic quest for self-realization and the potentially self-destructive quest for the secrets of the atom (CL 120).

Mirabell and his race fell as a result of their giving in to this will to nothingness. Previous to *Mirabell*, the "fall" in Merrill's poetry represents man's awakening into self-consciousness. Evil is seen as the necessary result of living, the product of experience itself. In *Mirabell*, we are given to understand that evil is the product of guilt. An agent with free will has chosen to defy or, by ignorance, has stumbled into defying the laws of an ordered universe. Mirabell says:

WE IMPLEMENT A SYSTEM
OF RULES WHICH GOVERN US & YOU   THESE NOT OBEYD WD GIVE
CHAOS A WEDGE &, NOT UNDERSTOOD, HAVE TURND OUR
LESSONS
THE COLOR OF CHAOS IN YR MINDS. (CL 246)

Even Mirabell's revelation that God B rules a determined world, in which no accident is allowed, fails to absolve its inhabitants of the responsibility of choice, as the members of his race experienced when they were punished for transgressing God B's law, even though their action ultimately contributed to his plan for the world.

Merrill is not always a consistent or convincing theologian. Although the spirits assert that "ABSOLUTES ARE NOW NEEDED" (CL 113), they seem unable or unwilling to be consistent in their espousal of which particular absolutes must be accepted. Their often contradictory assertions, troublesome in *Mirabell*, reach a near-cacophanous level in *Scripts*. Still, the general thrust of argument in *Mirabell* is clear, convincing, and consistently opposed to that of *Ephraim*. *Mirabell* is a world of rules and regulations. In this world, in which the narcissistic quest for the secret of the atom/Adam is forbidden, we come to know ourselves through the environmental restrictions that curtail the quest, our human limitations that—by restriction and reflection—allow us to gauge the lineaments of the self.

In *Ephraim*, the questers are concerned with limitations in a wholly negative fashion. They beat incessantly against the walls of human nature only to find themselves rebuffed time and again, resulting in responses such as "Higher than this I do not, dare not climb" (CL 71) and "Better to stop / While we still can" (CL 89). The questers' most daunting limitation in the earlier poem is time, whose power over mortal existence is repeatedly lamented, as in the poet's inclusion of a line from Heraclitus that might be read as a wry and self-pitying response to the entire poetic effort of *Ephraim*: "Time is a child, playing a board game: the kingdom of the child" (CL 60).

Mirabell calls time "A REGRESSIVE ANIMAL TRAIT" (CL 146). He says, "WE HAVE NO SENSE OF IT" (CL 146). The poet's Virgilian guide, W. H. Auden, responds to Mirabell's aversion to time and his loss of feeling by asking: "IS TIME THEN THE SOIL OF FEELING?" (CL 209). He concludes that Mirabell is striving to limit the questers' all-too-human concern with both time and feeling:

IT DAWNED (ON ME AT LEAST) THAT WE WERE BEING
EACH IN TURN STRIPPED   REDUCED TO ESSENCES
JOINED TO INFINITY (CL 209)

Mirabell supports this assertion by telling JM that:

> THE STRIPPING IS THE POINT YR POEM [*Ephraim*] WILL PERHAPS
> TAKE UP FROM ITS WINTRY END & MOVE STEP BY STEP INTO
> SEASONLESS & CHARACTERLESS STAGES TO ITS FINAL
> GREAT COLD RINGING OF THE CHIMES SHAPED AS 0 0 0 0 0 (CL211)

In *Ephraim*, the poet describes a similar "stripping process," but at that poem's "wintry end," JM is left feeling "chafed against, held cheap" (CL 89). Every major figure in the poem strives to strip the others of personality in a narcissistic economy of vicious individualism. JM reluctantly admits as much at the poem's conclusion, when he and DJ cannot rid themselves of the feeling that there is a "presence in [their] midst . . . unscrupulous to take what he can get" (CL 91).

In *Mirabell*, the loss of the self's autonomy is considered a gain. The questers in this poem are seeking to escape from self in favor of an absolute, which might be understood at various points in the poem as the absolute of tradition, of divine revelation, or of a form of community that includes many selves. The members of the community of *Mirabell* work together in their effort to wed mind and nature, sacrificing their individual selves in favor of the communal goal, the espousal of language as the great healer. They all are willing to be used, although JM and DJ have to be taught to see "use" as a benefit. Maria—one of the poet's dead friends who serves, together with Auden, as the questers' companion in the other world—explains how she has been "USED USED UTTERLY" in the service of this poem. JM asks her guiltily "What have we done to you, Maman?" only to be admonished "MES ENFANTS GET WISE: / TO BE USED HERE IS THE TRUE PARADISE" (CL 198).

This positive view of use allows JM finally to come to grips with the issue that plagues him throughout *Ephraim*, the "trade-off" between life and art. When DJ explains how the Ouija-board quest is making him feel more and more estranged from the real world, JM is "touched by his uncomplaining tone," and responds:

> What can I say? Nothing we haven't known.
> Remember Sam and Frodo in their hot
> Waterless desolation overshot
> By evil zombies. They of course come through
> —It's what, in any Quest, the heroes do—
> But at the cost of being set apart,
> Emptied, diminished. Tolkien knew this. Art—
> The tale that all but shapes itself—survives
> By feeding on its personages' lives.

> The stripping process, sort of. What to say?
> Our lives led *to* this. It's the price we pay. (CL 218)

JM admits that art "feeds" on life but insists that life is responsible for itself and that art is given free rein only at life's behest. The reference to J. R. R. Tolkien's elaborate tale of good and evil reminds us of the questers' responsibility to the community. Sam and Frodo are not alone in their threatened universe. They are acting on the part and for the good of their community.

The poet's consistent espousal of community in this poem opposes the romantic, Nietzschean notion so prominently felt in *Ephraim* that the truly strong self must divest itself of all ties to what is "other" in order to stand whole and uncompromised. The lesson of both *Mirabell* and *Ephraim* is that the single self is unknowable outside of a community, apart from its references. Auden reiterates this lesson and emphasizes the importance of a sense of *literary* community when he upbraids JM for complaining that the poem is "all by someone else. / In your voice, Wystan, or in Mirabell's" (CL 261):

> YR SCRUPLES DEAR BOY ARE INCONSEQUENT
> IF I MAY SAY SO   CAN U STILL BE BENT,
> AFTER OUR COURSE IN HOW TO SEE PAST LONE
> AUTONOMY TO POWERS BEHIND THE THRONE,
> ON DOING YR OWN THING: EACH TINY BIT
> (PARDON MME) MADE PERSONAL AS SHIT?
> GRANTED THAT IN 1ST CHILDHOOD WE WERE NOT
> PRAISED ENOUGH FOR GETTING OFF THE POT
> IT'S TIME TO DO SO NOW   THINK WHAT A MINOR
> PART THE SELF PLAYS IN A WORK OF ART
> COMPARED TO THOSE GREAT GIVENS   THE ROSEBRICK MANOR
> ALL TOPIARY FORMS & METRICAL
> MOAT ARIPPLE! (CL 262)

Auden's praise of the tradition that encases and enables any individual talent is echoed throughout the poem by a persistent undermining of the notion of individual autonomy. When Mirabell tells the questers that Ephraim was his pupil, DJ says that he had expected him to say that "Ephraim, too, was a composite / Voice," to which Mirabell responds, "HE IS THAT AS WELL   AS AM I MY FRIENDS   & AS YOU ARE" (CL 266). No single "voice" is entirely its own, as science has helped to prove. Mirabell says: "PHYSICISTS HAVE NOW DISCOVERD THERE IS NO NUMBER 1. / AS .999999999 IT TREMBLES / ON A DIGIT CENTRAL TO THEIR LOGIC" (CL 230). JM discovers this scientific questioning of individuality through his reading of modern scientific theory:

I lolled about one winter afternoon
In Stonington—rather, a whole precarious
Vocabulary of each different cell,
Enzyme, ion, what not, millionfold
(Down to the last bacterial organelle)
Particles that "show a tendency"
To form the person and the moods of me,
Lolled about. (CL 110)

The single self is composed of a community of selves, each with its own goals and directives. In this physical as well as spiritual sense, we are, each of us, more complicated than we might choose to believe. We are inextricably tied to the communities we inhabit and enhouse.

Auden is a natural teacher of this persuasion and a useful guide through *Mirabell.* His poetry is concerned with debunking the romantic myth of the autonomous, heroic self. He stands apart from the great modernist poets in English of our century as an espouser of community and civic duty above and beyond the creation of singular fictions. In his useful introduction to *Early Auden,* Edward Mendelson has argued that Auden sought to return poetry to a tradition in which the poet could once again speak from within a community. Mendelson has contended that romanticism set itself against the civic-minded poet of the eighteenth century; he argued that this romantic prejudice is evident "most strikingly in the large form of the quest":

Formerly an allegory of civil obligation, the quest now became the allegory of inner discontent. In civil literature, a quest hero ventured forth to seek a real goal that needed his presence. . . . But in literature that lacked external purpose, that had no audience that wanted it written, the quest, too, lost its tangible goals, and became compulsive and irresolute. The mad comic journey of Don Quixote was pursued in fatal earnest by the romantics. The price art paid for its autonomy was its desperate isolation. (xvii)

This is the isolation felt by the poet at the end of *Ephraim,* which might be thought of, in Mendelson's terms, as a failed attempt to create an epic poem, based on the expansion of the romantic lyric, that can speak for an entire community. Lyric-based epic fails as civic epic because it lacks any "external purpose" other than its own creation. The failure of *Ephraim* as a civic epic is not surprising. The poet of *Ephraim* is engaged in another task—the creation of a quest-romance revealing the lineaments of the individual poetic self. Quests such as this are not merely inner. They serve the community of readers through their revelation and recognition of the "inner adventure" (SP 32) upon which all of us are embarked, whether we recognize it or not. Nevertheless, the questing poet who would lead us through this adventure may become a prisoner of the very myopic vision that has allowed him to banish the outer world for the sake of the inner one. Once this happens, the poet is forced to turn his vision outward or else abandon his quest for revelation.

Early on in *Mirabell,* Merrill announces his intention to write a poem opposed to the myopic, centripetal, and lyric-based *Ephraim*:

> This is not an act
> Calling for timeskip and gadabout,
> Like *Ephraim*. But one benefit of doubt,
> As of credulity, is its tiresomeness.
> Let ours, then, be the first thing I suppress,
> Or try to.
> ....
> There's no choice, really. Don't think we *decide* (CL 114–15)

This passage enables us to make two important points about the nature of *Mirabell* that allow us to characterize it as a civic epic. It reminds us that *Mirabell* is a continuous narrative, with little of the lyrical "timeskip and gadabout" of *Ephraim*. The last line also informs us that the poet has adopted a passive position in relation to an acknowledged absolute—the revelation that he is being compelled to deliver to a waiting audience. The two points are interconnected. Narrative is inherently other-based. The narrator places himself in a subservient position to his narration and, by extension, to his audience.

The form of narrative implies that there is a story worth telling and an audience that is willing to listen; it is a public mode of discourse. Lyric poetry, by contrast, has all of the characteristics of a private utterance, of the poet talking to himself or, at most, to his self-reflected environment (including the like-minded reader). In *Ephraim,* the narrative is discontinuous and layered. Story-lines are picked up and dropped without warning, and narration is often foregone altogether in favor of densely symbolic lyric. Several of the narrative lines, especially that of the lost novel, are nearly incomprehensible on a first reading. The lyric-based, discontinuous narrative style of *Ephraim* serves to emphasize the personality of the poet behind the poem, since he is the one constant upon which the reader might rely. The difficult style of the poem contributes to its major theme: the difficulty and final impossibility of knowing or defining the autonomous self.

Mirabell, by contrast, is narrative-based. Lyrics are interspersed throughout. These serve neither to interrupt nor further the narrative so much as to accent a particular theme. In this sense, the lyrics in

Mirabell serve much the same purpose as the aria in Italian opera or the song in Shakespearean drama. The narrative itself is carried forward by the conversation between DJ and JM and the Ouija-board figures. It proceeds at a chatty, leisurely pace that is easily followed.

Merrill's decision to switch from a lyric-based poem with a discontinuous narrative to an almost wholly narrative poem with occasional lyrics has broad ramifications. Narrative is inherently teleological; all characters and personalities within a narrative are made finally subordinate to the completion of the narrative itself. In the previous chapter, we located the major narrative of *Ephraim* outside of the actual poem, in its composition by the poet. In this manner, the poet was able to place personality in a superior position to written narrative and still maintain a functional narrative form. The personality of the poet of *Mirabell* is placed firmly within the confines of the poem itself, which is enlarged both in scope and in literal number of pages to make room.

Since the poet has given up the revelation of his own personality as an end in itself, we must look elsewhere for the telos of *Mirabell*. When we do so, we find that the poem's composition is given primacy. The purpose of this composition is not to reveal the identity of the poet, as in *Ephraim*, but to address an audience. *Ephraim* begins with a strong sense of audience and of urgency: "The baldest prose / Reportage was called for" (CL 3). But the sense of a waiting audience is lost in the ensuing poem's difficult, lyric maze. In *Mirabell*, after JM is told that he is to write poems of science, he consoles himself by asserting "the few of more than common sense—/ Who but they would be our audience?" (CL 109). This acute awareness of audience is present throughout the poem.

In the simplest sense, the audience in *Mirabell* is the reader of the poem, and the player is the poet who has been instructed to deliver his material in the best manner possible. This player-poet might be likened to a teacher or a prophet who has received the message: "MAKE GOD OF SCIENCE / TELL OF POWER" (CL 113). Through his divinely inspired message, the poet as prophet is to convince man to "LOVE HIS MIND & LANGUAGE" (CL 121). Since the poet is continually present in the poem as a disciple of higher powers, we may easily forget that this poem is the product of his shaping hand, and that we—as audience—are responsible for judging the play (or poem) before us. We are likely to feel ourselves akin to the poet as fellow pilgrims and students. From this position of subservience, we receive the messages from Mirabell and his cohorts as divine revelations. As readers, we occupy a dual position. We are, at once, ignorant pilgrims and judging audience. Our dual role as readers is mirrored by the author's dual personality in the poem. Merrill's "JM," like Proust's "Marcel," is both the author-narrator and the author's fictional character.

None of this is new or surprising information about the nature of a first-person narrative, but I have risked stating the obvious in order to make a general assertion about the particular nature of this poem. I contend that Mirabell's revelations, which we, along with the fictional character of the poet, receive as ignorant pilgrims, are often to be distrusted, if not discounted, as being self-serving rationalizations that are being put forward in defense of the poet's life history.

In the previous chapter, I refer to *Ephraim* as a poem of mid-life crisis, in which the poet is seeking to defend the manner in which he has led his life. The poet is particularly concerned with defending his position as a poet from charges made by his family, lovers, and friends that they have been compromised for the sake of the creative process. In *Mirabell*, the poet is continuing his defense, not against family and friends but against society at large, the focus of this civic quest. In defending himself against society, this poet, whose lifework has been concerned primarily with private loves and losses, finds himself making an essentially elitist argument. Readers may well be offended.

The poet has several factors in his favor, however. This elitist argument is not strictly his but is in the voice of the revealing spirits, being revealed to the character JM. The reader will perceive that the spirits' unabashed elitism is countered by their kind and gracious treatment of the subservient quester and, by extension, of the reader himself. One might argue that the questers and spirits form an elite of their own, and such an argument is certainly supported by the spirits' dogma. But the basic civility practiced by all major participants in the poem helps to overcome, though not account for, the distaste a reader may feel for the poem's elitist dogma. The poem's major theme, concerning the indivisibility of mind and nature, is better represented by the spirits' civility than by their questionable dogma.

The spirits' distasteful dogma is not unfounded. Their directives concerning birth control, atomic energy, and the environment are all sensible reactions to our most pressing global needs. Nevertheless, when Mirabell asserts that "THE LAST USE FOR RELIGION" is "TO KEEP AT SWORDSPOINT / THE GREAT FACTIONS OF EAST & WEST SO THAT LESSR POWERS / FACING MASS STARVATION WILL BE DISTRACTED FROM DROPPING / ATOMIC BOMBS TO GET FOOD" (CL 193), we may feel justifiably uncomfortable with the self-serving nature of the "revelation." Similarly, Mirabell's assertion that "WE

CLONE THE HAPPY FEW THE MASSES WE NEED / NEVER CONSIDER THEY REMAIN IN AN ANIMAL STATE" (CL 188) could easily set us squirming (as it does DJ and Auden in the poem). An artistic or literary elitism is easily defended. But, when this elitism is transferred to a universal level, the political danger cannot be discounted—indeed, it is accepted as inevitable by Mirabell—that such justified elitism may be used as an apology for totalitarianism. Mirabell attempts to defend the usefulness of totalitarianism, arguing that "THE HITLERS THE PERONS & FRANCOS . . . / ARE NEEDED" (CL 188). He defends such politically suspect statements by telling JM that his poem, like Dante's politically obsessed *Comedy*, "MAY NEED TO BE MADE UP WITH . . . DIRTY SHEETS" (CL 188). But Dante's intense political convictions cannot be compared seriously to this poem's offhand defense of dictatorship. Merrill lacks a strong political sensibility. When he attempts to make a political argument, he is usually at his weakest. One is not led to question this poet's politics, as with Eliot or Yeats. Rather, we question his wisdom in making a political argument at all, given his temperamental diffidence before the subject. We might compare Merrill's casually naive political self to the queen in Firbank's *The Flower Beneath the Foot*. When informed that her political opinions might be called into question, she cavalierly responds, "No one knows what my political opinions are; I don't myself!" (207).

Merrill again argues from an elitist perspective when contending that the gay, childless artist is superior to his straight counterpart. This argument concerns an artistic rather than a universal elite, but we may still feel that Mirabell's teachings on this account are conveniently self-serving. Mirabell's justification for a homosexual artistic elite is based upon his race's general bias for mind over nature.

> LOVE OF ONE MAN FOR ANOTHER OR LOVE BETWEEN WOMEN
> IS A NEW DEVELOPMENT OF THE PAST 4000 YEARS
> ENCOURAGING SUCH MIND VALUES AS PRODUCE THE BLOSSOMS
> OF POETRY AND MUSIC, THOSE 2 PRINCIPAL LIGHTS OF
> GOD BIOLOGY. LESSR ARTS NEEDED NO EXEGETES:
> ARCHITECTURE SCULPTURE THE MOSAICS & PAINTINGS THAT
> FLOWERD IN GREECE & PERSIA CELEBRATED THE BODY.
> POETRY MUSIC SONG INDWELL & CELEBRATE THE MIND . . .
> HEART IF U WILL (CL 156)

Mirabell's praise of homosexuality is based on its being "un-natural." Like Plato, he prefers to think of homosexual love as being a spiritual and not a physical union, an ideal love that rises above the carnal to the realm of enlightenment: "NOW MIND IN ITS PURE FORM IS A NONSEXUAL PASSION / OR A UNISEXUAL ONE PRODUCING

ONLY LIGHT" (CL 156). This world of light is deemed superior to any "natural" world composed of the four elements—earth, air, fire and water—and of the pigments that produce colors when light is shone upon them (CL 215):

NATURE MEASURED ON THE FAIR SCALES OF
LIGHT
IS OF AN INFERIOR RANK SHE & HER ELEMENTS
WD FAIL WITHOUT LIGHT & ITS COLORS, AS WE WHO APPROACH
THE DWELLING PLACE OF LIGHT NOW BEGIN TO SEE (CL 230)

The one requirement that Mirabell stresses as necessary for making this quest to enlightenment is not homosexuality but "CHILDLESSNESS": "THIS TURNS US / OUTWARD TO THE LESSONS & THE MYSTERIES" (CL 216).

Once again, we enter the world of "The Broken Home" where Merrill first considered how he was to make up for the child he would never have. From the beginning, he viewed his poetry as a substitute for this unborn child, a substitute that has the added benefit of being bodiless, mind-born, and eternal. In *Mirabell,* he draws a parallel between his creation of poems, which bring together mind and matter, and the twin Egyptian rulers' (Akhnaton and Nefertiti) worship of the sun, of which Mirabell says: "THEY LITERALLY HARNESSED MATTER / WITH THE REINS OF THE SUN" (CL 227). These legendary ruler-gods are said to have built an enormous crystal pyramid with which to harness the sun's power, but the capstone was minutely flawed, "ITS GRAIN VARIED JUST ENOUGH TO SAVE THE WORLD" (CL 227). Without that flaw, the sun's captured power would have created an explosion to rival that caused by a nuclear bomb (CL 127).

The search for enlightenment can lead to self-destruction, as the questers discover near the end of *Ephraim*. What saves the creating self from the destructive power of the unmitigated light of "pure" mind is "the grain / Of imperfection in that quartz capstone, / The human mind—Akhnaton's or our own" (CL 227). The questers in *Mirabell,* far from lamenting their inability to become one with the absolute, as in *Ephraim,* recognize that it is this very inability that saves them from self-destruction. What remains from encounters with the absolute are the spoils of art, the rewards of a "REASONED INDIRECTION" (CL 242) by which we seek enlightenment without being destroyed by our discoveries. Akhnaton and Nefertiti discovered that humans cannot stand very much reality when they "FOCUSD" their crystal pyramid "ON ONE / GLOWING UNIFYING VISION" (CL 242), and they nearly destroyed the world.

Because of this disaster, God B determined that artists and scientists, not political or religious leaders, would have to prepare the way to paradise. Mirabell seems to be arguing, like Christ, against the notion of an earthly paradise—at least for our time. Instead, the poet, musician, and scientist—those creators most devoted to an ideal rather than to nature—must point the way to a future world of perfection. The childless artist, like the childless priest, represents, by his sacrificing of the natural world, the aspiration to a higher, brighter sphere of spiritual perfection. In *Mirabell*, we are given to understand that procreation is the necessary result of our fall from a higher world of changeless perfection. The urge to procreate is viewed as being synonymous with the urge to violate the single atom—the image of inviolability in an ideal world—through nuclear fission:

> [Mirabell's] whole point's the atom's
> Precarious inviolability.
> Eden tells a parable of fission,
> Lost world and broken home, the bitten apple
> Stripped of its seven veils, nakedness left
> With no choice but to sin and multiply.
> From then on, genealogical chain reactions
> Ape the real thing. (CL 192)

By remaining childless, the artist pits himself against the fallen world of nature, which uses procreation to repeat the image of man "AS IN / A DISTORTING MIRROR" (CL 229). The childless artist seeks to reveal an undistorted vision of unfallen man. His very childlessness places this task before him, as the legend of Akhnaton and Nefertiti serves to illustrate:

> AFTER PRODUCING 5 STILL BORN MONSTERS
> THEY SAW THEIR LOVE DOOMD TO GIVE BIRTH TO IDEAS
> ALONE.
> LIKE APHRODITE FROM THE WATERS ROSE THEIR WORSHIP OF
> THE SUN (CL 225)

Their sterile condition forced these rulers to turn to the light of ideas. Their discovery of the ideal is made parallel in this passage to the birth of the goddess of love, Venus/Aphrodite.

Merrill leads us in the previous poem to view Ephraim (whose name in the lost novel is "Eros") as the product, sometimes regretted, of the relationship between JM and DJ. Mirabell presents the questers with much the same reasoning for his own incarnation when he explains: "THIS FIELD IS FORMD BY LONGSTANDING EXPERIENCE / . . . DJ's and Mine? / YES" (CL 253). Like Ephraim, Mirabell is the issue of JM's and DJ's union. We might qualify this statement by saying that Mirabell, *in his transfigured form*, is the product of this union. JM's and DJ's devotion to his unlovable, bat-like self enables Mirabell to experience the transforming power of love as he metamorphoses into a peacock.

Mirabell's "appearance" is visible only to the mind's eye. The spirits inform JM that they see nothing themselves except through his imagination. Mirabell's transformation, then, must be regarded as a change of mind or heart within the poet himself. When we recall the major lesson of *Mirabell*—that mind *is* matter, as fact is fable—we see that Mirabell's transformation is more than a mood swing within the poet; or *if* a mood swing, then one that must be understood as changing the very nature of reality. Mind and nature are hopelessly intertwined. Their insoluble marriage is well represented by the incarnation of Mirabell as a "peacock," for, as Bachelard has remarked, "the eye of the [peacock's] feather is also called its *mirror*. This is a new proof of the ambivalence which plays about the two participles *seen* and *seeing*" (WD 29). In the world of *Mirabell*, subject and object are unfixed categories, fluctuating and interchangeable. Mirabell's transformation is both the product and proof of the love between JM and DJ.

Both this love and its product are "Platonic," as Mirabell informs us when asking JM, "IS THE PEACOCK NOT ALSO SOMEWHAT ATHENIAN?" (CL 158), by which JM and DJ assume he means both "gay" and "devoted to an ideal." Merrill is almost assuredly referring to the passage in the *Symposium* in which Diotima explains to Socrates that children born of the union of two souls are "fairer and more immortal" than children of the body (200). These children of the soul ensure the parents' immortality. Mirabell's transformation and the poem describing this transformation represent a spiritual and moral victory for the poet. As Mirabell's bat self represents the danger of the absurd and the loss of feeling for JM, so his peacock self represents a new beginning, a spiritual rebirth enabled by the acceptance of human limitation.

This acceptance of limitation can be seen throughout the poem in the characters' respect for manners and courtesy. Mirabell's predecessors, present at the poem's beginning, are unmannered; they fail to show respect for the questers' human limitations and are quickly replaced. JM's demand that the spirits treat him with civility, respecting his human limitations without being patronizing, results in the arrival of Mirabell, who displays the humility of the well-mannered:

> I AM A MERE MIXING AGENT   WITH MY SUPERIORS
> U WD HAVE LEARNED FASTER BUT NOT IN TURN MADE AS WE

HAVE
THIS WORLD OF COURTESY
Breaking off, the cup strolls round the Board
As who should take a deep breath before speaking:
NOR WD I HAVE COME TO LOVE U
Love us? Sudden garlands (the tin ceiling's)
Swim into focus. Then you do have feelings! (CL 155)

Mirabell's return of feelings, based on his experience of "this world of courtesy," complements JM's loss of negative and self-destructive feelings. *Ephraim* had left JM feeling "piercingly / Aware of . . . black holes in me: / Waste, self-hatred, boredom. One by one / These weeks here at the Board, they've been erased" (CL 187). JM is restored by the civility of the world of *Mirabell*. Like Mirabell, he becomes "FILLED WITH . . . MANNERS" (CL 155), which we might define here as the guidelines by which one comes to respect the limitations of self and others.

It is fitting that the literary model Merrill takes for this comedy of manners is the most highly "mannered" of dramatic forms, the court masque. His use of the masque serves to illustrate his poem's main theme, the marriage of mind and nature or, to put it another way, the indivisibility of fact and fable. In his book on the Jonsonian masque, Stephen Orgel, whom Merrill cites as an influence (REC 65), has argued that the masque symbolizes the wedding of the ideal to the real made manifest in the moment when the masquers move "from the stage into the world of the court" (149), from the dramatic world of the antimasque, "a world of particularity and mutability—of accidents," to the masque proper, a world inhabited by "ideal abstractions and eternal verities" (73). The court masque as metaphor points to the possibility of moving *through* the realm of appearance into the world of essence. This "essential" masque world is a world of Platonic forms that do not oppose the physical world of appearance but supersede it.

JM and DJ have to be taught to value this unseen world, to look for the essence behind appearance and the fable behind fact. Early in the poem, when the spirits are relating their mythical history to JM, he responds: "Surely underneath such fables lie / Facts far more thrilling—won't you specify?" (CL 121). Near the poem's conclusion, Auden corrects JM's mistake of placing facts in the superior position to fable:

FACTS JM WERE ALL U KNEW TO WANT.
WRETCHED RICKETY RECALCITRANT
URCHINS, THE FEW WHO LIVE GROW UP TO BE
IMPS OF THE ANTIMASQUE RUDE SCENERY
& GUTTURAL STOMPINGS, WHEN THE SOVREIGN NODS,
SOUNDLESSLY DIVIDE & HERE A TABLE

IS SET & LAMPS FOR THE FEASTING GODS
OBERON'S COURT (OR MY FRIEND'S CAVE) APPEARS.
THE ELDER FACTS IN LIVERY OF FABLE
HAVE JOINED THE DANCE (CL 263)

Although Plato's cave and Oberon's court do not belong to the world of appearance, they are more real than the facts (imps of the anti-masque) that we mistakenly call reality. Only facts that have been sufficiently mythologized, those upon which the livery of fable has been bestowed, can justifiably be called real.

Once more we are reminded of Bachelard's placement of noumena in the superior position to phenomena; we may even recall Hippolyta's famous rebuke to Theseus' demeaning of imagination in *A Midsummer Night's Dream*:

All their minds transfigur'd so together,
More witnesseth than fancy's images,
And grows to something of great constancy;
But howsoever, strange and admirable. (5.1.24–27)

The great constant is the lovers' story itself—or, to take a step backwards in perspective—the play in which their story is told. In Merrill's poem, the character of Mirabell is the constant: He is the "MIRACLE" and the "MIRAGE" (CL 236), the representative of the transforming power of metaphor—the magic of man's mind. As he says, "MAKE OF ME THE PROCESS SOMEWHERE / OPERATING BETWEEN TREE & PULP & PAGE & POEM" (CL 173).

Mirabell's position as the transforming agent is further defined when he announces, "THE TRANSFORMING & DELIVERY / OF SOULS, OURS: WE ARE MERCURY" (CL 246). Mercury, like Plato's Eros, Dante's Amore, and the spirit Ephraim, represents the potentially divine element in man. The major component of the masque—the transformation from the fallen, mutable world to the world of eternal forms—is represented in potentiality in the figure of Mercury. Another name for Mercury is quicksilver, the substance once used as the reflective backing on mirrors. The world of appearances and the possibility of seeing *through* appearance both exist as potential in the symbolic figure of Mercury.

The incarnation of Mercury is the first step in bringing together the worlds of noumena and phenomena, fable and fact. This incarnation is symbolized by the advent of language, by which thoughts become facts and facts become thoughts. Mercury, or "reflection," or language bridges the gap between an individual mind and the other. It creates reality to fill this gap. From the opposite point of view, we might say that the reflecting mind, embodied in language, *creates* the gap by forcing a space for itself in the universe.

Merrill presents this complex notion of the creation and filling of the space between the self and other as a "rupture" caused by a mirror, by Mercury. In typical fashion, he domesticates the entire process by representing this rupture between the self and other as the actual, physical rupture DJ sustains when carrying a heavy, gold-framed mirror up the stairs (CL 163). This mirror is the very source of reflection and of the appearances that separate us from the essential world of forms. But the rupture that the mirror causes is also, Mirabell says, the "DUES" that "ADMIT" JM and DJ "TO THE SEMINAR" (CL 163). The mirror stands for this mutable world, with all of its pains and joys. As the representative of limitation in our mutable world of appearances, it conversely symbolizes the possibility of transformation and metamorphosis.

While stressing rules and regulations, Mirabell repeatedly reminds the questers of the potential inherent in human limitation. When JM laments that human beings cannot escape the prison-house of reflection—"If only we were less free to reflect; / If diametrics of the mirror didn't / Confirm the antiface there as one's own"—Mirabell responds with an equivocal "YES NO PERHAPS," but he then reminds JM of the world outside of his limited reflection: "WE ARE MOVING TOWARD THE GREAT DOORS" (CL 163). The poet is more interested here in the potential evidenced by limitation than by limitation itself (his obsession in *Ephraim*), as is made evident when he responds to Mirabell's revelation that he is Mercury:

> With new eyes we confront the mirror,
> Look *beyond* ourselves. Does he appear?
> Never plainer, never more hidden, his glassy
> Foyer, his permeable impasse.
> Reason might argue that to enforce our absence
> Upon it wipes the gleaming slab
> Of him as well. Instead, this quasi-
> Liverish cloud betrays
> A presence hitherto unseen; (CL 249)

Unseen because unlooked for. Potential is apparent to the beholder who wishes to believe in "something of great constancy," which is finally unprovable, a matter of faith.

Mirabell's "appearance" is a case in point. We have remarked that he appears only in the mind's eye; Maria notes, "HE APPEARS IN US OUR MINDS (HEARTS) ARE HIS MIRROR" (CL 157). When the mind ceases to believe, Mirabell is robbed of his appearance: "OUR

PEACOCK IS DEMOTED JUST THE DIM / EXPOSURE OF A ONCE BLACK SHAPE WITH WINGS / Because we doubted him? Ah, it's not fair!" (CL 177). Mirabell's return to his "once black shape" is a reminder of the fallen, atomic world he represents and also of his fallen race, which was damned for failing to believe in the integrity of the single atom/Adam. The question of belief is weighted in this volume with the awful potential for self-destruction in this skeptical nuclear age.

Nonetheless, Mirabell also symbolizes salvation. His transformation from bat to peacock may be thought of in masque terms as the transition from anti-masque to masque, from the world of mere appearance to the world of idealized forms. In this masque world, which the questers enter with the transformation of Mirabell, there is "NO ACCIDENT," a "BASIC PRECEPT" that Mirabell tells the questers they must take on faith (CL 179). Such a doctrine is necessary if we are to view our lives, and history itself, as quest-narratives, in which the "ENTIRE APPARATUS" develops "THE WAY TO PARADISE" (CL 180). The inherent implication of the teleological narrative form is that it could have happened no other way. Toward the end of *Mirabell*, the questers' friend, Robert Morse, remarks upon reading the unfinished manuscript of the poem: "Ephraim had to lead / Precisely here" (CL 256). The alternative model, which we might call the "lyric" model of history, is circular. In lyric-based epic, the sublime is found and lost repeatedly, as we witnessed in *Ephraim*. In *Mirabell*, the "truth" of romantic lyric—that paradise may be found or glimpsed in the moment of the intersection of the timeless with time—is not abandoned; rather, it is incorporated into a linear model of progress toward a real paradise in the real future. If we recall our discussion of "The Broken Home," in which we remarked upon the "masculine" nature of linearity and the "feminine" nature of circularity, then we see how Merrill's merging of the circular lyric with linear narrative might be considered a "marriage" of masculine mind with feminine nature.

The apt symbol for this narrative is the spiral, representing the marriage of the linear and the circular. Early on in *Mirabell*, JM attempts to quell DJ's fears about the nature of their new spiritual guides by invoking the image of the spiral quest:

you're dead right, it
is scary. But so, don't forget was Ephraim
at first. Say we've reached again some relative
point—that of fear—on a spiral forever
widening. Why couldn't the whole adventure

> *as before, just graze peril on its outward*
> *curve to insight?* (CL 111)

The spiral is at once a stair ascending to infinity and a drill bit boring down into human nature. The two quests are the same, and the vision of life as a spiral quest is hard-wired into human nature.

This implication is made clear when the poet describes the DNA molecule in section 6 as a spiral map, a huge model of which he has studied at the Boston Museum of Science:

> Even grossly simplified, as here,
> It's too much. Who by reference to this
> 3-D map's infernal skeins
> And lattices could hope to find his way?
> Yet, strange to say, that's just what everyone
> On Earth is promptly known for having done. (CL 203)

As with Auden's paean to tradition, this reference to DNA serves to undermine our typical notions of individuality and free will. The poet of *Mirabell* is less concerned with lamenting human limitation than with marveling at human life itself. He finds reassurance in the very complexity and grace of our determined, "spiral" natures.

The questers of *Mirabell* are content with understanding and praising life's pageant. Indeed, "questers" may not be a very accurate label for JM and DJ in this volume, in which they are repeatedly referred to as students and patients. Perhaps we would do best to consider them initiates into Mirabell's brand of radical humanism. Mirabell is a thorough-going humanist whose declared purpose is to "MAKE MAN THE CLONE OF GOD" (CL 269). Again we are reminded of the fitting parallel between this poem and *The Magic Flute,* in which Sarastro's realm is meant to prepare the initiates for the time when "earth will be a realm of heaven, / and mortals will be like gods" (198). Mirabell is this poem's Sarastro, leading JM and DJ through a series of initiation and purification rites toward their "RELEASE INTO LIGHT" (CL 234).

The transformation of the questers of *Ephraim* into the initiates of *Mirabell* is represented well by Merrill's reversal of the "fishing" metaphor that he employs in *Ephraim* when describing his first contact with the dead on the Ouija board: "One more try. / Was anybody there? As when a pike / Strikes, and the line singing writes in lake-flesh / Highstrung runes, and reel spins and mind reels / YES a new and urgent power YES / Seized the cup" (CL 6). In *Mirabell,* DJ and JM are the "catch":

(Why not, deep down, admit we're hooked? I make
These weak signs of resistance for form's sake,
Testing the tautness of the line whereby
We're drawn—tormented spangles, I now guess,
The measure of our mounting shallowness—
Willy-nilly towards some high and dry
Ecstasy, a light we trust will neither
Hurt nor kill but permeate its breather.
One wants to have been thought worth fighting for,
And not be thrown back, with a shrug, from shore.) (CL 138)

The initiates' journey towards the shallows and into light is represented in the poem as a journey through the basic "elements," of which all life is composed, and into the light, which is the giver of life (CL 210). The "elements" represent nature, as "light" represents mind. The initiates' trials in the elements on their way to the light of pure mind may be viewed as part of the effort to wed mind and nature. In leading the questers to enlightenment *through* nature, Mirabell is guarding against the false sublime, the self-deceiving divorce of nature from mind.

Mirabell's transformation into a peacock is proof of the initiates' initial success at wedding mind to nature. As befits the static, anti-dramatic character of a masque, Mirabell's actual metamorphosis occurs off-stage, but homage is paid to it in nine seven-line stanzas of verse, the last three stanzas being spoken by the "elements" (earth, air, fire, and water), of which Mirabell—and all life—is composed. Speaking to the assembled initiates (JM, DJ, Auden, and Maria), the elements say of Mirabell:

YOUR PEACOCK'S WINGS

WE PAINTED, HIS SPREAD TAIL & SAPPHIRE BREAST,
BUT YOUR MINDS COALESCED
TO FORM HIS: HE IS YOURS. MIND HAS THIS FORCE,
IS DEATHLESS, IS THE MUSIC DANTE HEARD,
THE ENERGY WE DRAW FROM MANIFEST
IN 5 RINGS ROUND THE SOURCE (CL 161)

We all represent within ourselves the marriage of mind and nature, with mind like a planet at the invisible center of our being, surrounded by its elemental embodiment. A continual dialogue between mind and body may be felt within each of us, between the deathless spirit and its embodying, enabling elements. What Mirabell calls "V" work is the outer manifestation of this dialogue best expressed in culture's "ENTIRE LIFE-FABRIC WOVEN OF LANGUAGE" (CL 241). Language is the outer expression of the essential paradox of human life—the marriage of the invisible spirit to the visible body—since language is composed of mind-born concepts and natural images.

All images are natural, but the most powerful of images (and those given primacy throughout *Mirabell* and *Scripts*) are those firmly grounded in the four elements: earth, air, fire, and water. Through these elements, of which we are composed, we are linked integrally to the world around us. Merrill's conception of the primacy of elemental images seems to be borrowed from Bachelard's concept of the material-based imagination, which is centered upon the four elements:

> I am justified in characterizing the four elements as the hormones of the imagination. They activate groups of images. They help in assimilating inwardly the reality that is dispersed among forms. They bring about the great syntheses that are capable of giving somewhat regular characteristics to the imaginary. (AD 11)

Elemental images "speak" to us, according to Bachelard, at depths we cannot measure rationally. Poetry alone of written languages has the power to gauge the intuitive weight of these images, since poetic language is language untied from its rational concept. The poet believes in the power of the unspoken, the elemental image that is felt before it is understood. Poetic language remains always one step ahead of the *merely* rational; by so doing, it allows the individual a glimpse of freedom and possibility. "Un-poetic" language, by contrast, is in perpetual danger of losing the natural image upon which it is based, of becoming "un-material." Language that has lost its material image represents a mind estranged from nature, imprisoned in sterile, mind-forged conceptions. Such unnatural, unpoetic language serves to threaten the tenuous marriage between mind and nature, between the self and other.

The elements that spoke above refer to this dangerous, unproductive language when they warn JM against anti-matter:

> ONE CAUTIONARY WORD:
>
> THE MATTER WHICH IS NOT WAS EVER OURS
> TO GUARD AGAINST. ITS POWERS
> ARE MAGNETIZED BY FOREIGN BEACONS, BLACK
> HANDS TESTING THE GREENHOUSE PANE BY PANE.
>
> CLING TO YOUR UNION: 5 THRU THE DARK HOURS
> WE KEEP WATCH WE PRESS BACK. (CL 161)

The "greenhouse" is our natural world, which, according to Mirabell's elaborate materialist myth, is both a single cell (CL 210) and God himself (CL 187). Mirabell's implied plea for restraint by atomic scientists is also a warning against the poet's acquiescence to the "false sublime" and the layman's discounting of things not seen.

The initiates of *Mirabell* have to be taught the value of seeing things "both ways," or even three or four ways. Near the beginning of the poem, JM expresses impatience with the bats' materialist myth by which they equate their race's history with the nature of matter. JM recognizes that these fables must have some deeply personal meaning, which he is as yet unable to fathom. In exasperation, he tells the spirits to

> Speak without metaphor.
> Help me to drown the double-entry book
> I've kept these fifty years. You want from me
> Science at last, instead of tapestry—
> Then tell me round what brass tack the old silk frays.
> Stop trying to have everything both ways.
> It's too much to be batwing angels *and*
> Inside the atom, don't you understand? (CL 122)

JM's reluctance to accept metaphor from the spirits indicates a fundamental distrust of language and hearkens back to his frustration in *Ephraim* with his inability to translate his feelings into words. Mirabell responds by arguing that feelings and personality exist only insofar as language can describe them. We cannot get beyond language to a final reality underneath, and, if we strive to do so, we will find ourselves face to face with the absurd. Mirabell instructs his initiates to avoid false ideals, such as the quest for a language without metaphor. He wants them to understand the nature of language itself.

Language is a gift of environment—of heredity, history, society, and culture—by dint of which the spoken or written self is an inherently public self. Without language to reflect the self, there would be no self to reflect. Mirabell describes his pre-language existence:

> B4 OUR MEETING I WAS NOTHING NO TIME PASSD BUT NOW
> YR TOUCH LIKE A LAMP HAS SHOWN ME TO MYSELF & I AM
> ME. . . I HAVE ENTERD A GREAT WORLD I AM FILLD
> WITH IS IT MANNERS? (CL 155)

Yes, manners and morals and feelings and virtues and vices—all of which Mirabell's kind cannot recognize or possess, since they "HAVE NEVER EXPRESSD A THING" (CL 172).

Man is of a different order. His "soul" connects him to the divine, and, when he creates, using language, he in fact becomes a god, fashioning something from nothing. The most godlike of mankind's creations is music, which is "MORE ABSTRACT / THAN METAPHOR" (CL 206) and thus more "essential" than the written word. Written language requires the rational mind's necessarily deforming recognition of nonrational images. Words require understanding, which implies the possibility—or rather, the inevitability—of error. God as the ideal creator lacks the "human volubility" that leads to error. He "*Has* no word for His own power and grace," and "left alone, just falls back on flimflam / Tautologies like *I am that I am* / Or *The world is everything that is the case*" (CL 223). The initiates agree that music is the supreme creative art, being "LIKE TIME / RETOLD . . . / A WAY OF TELLING THAT INSPIRES BELIEF" (CL 206). Music requires no participation from the rational, erring mind.

The written language that aspires most successfully to the condition of music is the most irrational of written languages, poetry. When the composer or poet uses his language to inspire belief in the listener or reader, he is offering proof of his faith in the unseen, in the possibility of creating something from nothing. By the same token, we are given to understand that any exploration of the nature of poetry or of music is likewise an attempt to define the nature of belief.

As we read through *Mirabell* and into *Scripts*, we find Merrill more and more concerned with exploring and defining his poetics, as well as his system of belief. His attempts to display the abstract entities upon which poetic images are based might be considered, in this sense, as trials of faith. These image builders come in fives: the four elements, with the "shaping hand" of nature; the four colors—red, blue, yellow, and green—which merge into white; the four seasons and one sun, which, through photosynthesis, stores a "NEAT 5TH SEASON" in the "GREEN LEAF" (CL 230); and our five senses. These senses serve as the link between the "physical" and the "soul," between nature and mind, and so are the very tie that binds in that marriage (CL 230). The elements, colors, and seasons comprise the physical world in which we live. Our five senses' perception of these in images connect the soul to the world as to the body. The image itself serves as the symbol of this otherwise invisible union of soul and world, mind and nature, and the *making* of a poetic image is a sign of faith in that union.

The poet's "studies" in the basic "fives" of which images are comprised are embodied in his works, in his projections onto the world of no appearance, the unseen world on the other side of the mirror. JM sees the connection between faith and works as being embodied in the imaginative passage through the mirror, the metamorphosis of the self into other: "we / Like Stanislavsky's actors, try to *be* / The rose, the ingot . . . Empathy is art" (CL 224). As JM strives to delve into the nature of color, Wystan and Maria change colors by changing clothes in the imaginative mirror-world of the poem. Maria gives up the unadorned black that was her trademark in life and gradually moves from color to color of the spectrum on the way to white. She serves as a materialist metaphor for the initiates' gradual purification in their progress to the light of pure mind. When the initiates "fail" in their trials by losing faith in their color-coated peacock, Mirabell—the central image in this poem of the power of the imagination, which weds possibility to necessity—Wystan and Maria disappear, returning to the black along with the peacock, which metamorphoses into a black bat (CL 234).

Metamorphosis is at the very heart of this poem. Far from bemoaning change, as in *Ephraim*, the poet here revels in the potential for transformation embodied in the dialectic between mind and nature, possibility and necessity, masque and anti-masque. Implied in the metamorphosis theme is the impossibility of ever making a certain distinction between appearance and reality, the self as actor and the self as audience. The idea that life is a "fond pageant" in which we as players migrate constantly between one side of the proscenium arch and the other, without ever knowing exactly in which position we stand, lies as firmly behind *Mirabell* as it does behind *A Midsummer Night's Dream*.

The relationship of audience to player as trope in this poem is complex. In one respect, JM and DJ are the audience watching a play spelled out on the Ouija board, which they have set up on a white, round-topped dining-room table:

> our table's white
> Theatre in the round fills, dims . . . Crosslight
> From YES and NO dramatically picks
> Four figures out. And now the twenty-six
> Footlights, arranged in semicircle, glow.
> What might be seen as her "petit noyau"
> By Mme Verdurin assembles at
> Stage center (CL 147)

Compared to this elaborate stage production of dead friends and cosmic spirits, the "real world" appears diminished to JM and DJ, a mere "safety door / Left open onto light. Too small, too far / To help. The blind bright spot of where we are" (CL 148).

The closing line indicates that the questers are not only audience but also players, lit up by the "blind bright spot" of supernatural attention. Their dead friends and familiar spirits comprise an audience of their own, as they look toward the mirror in which DJ and JM appear, for entertainment and for enlightenment. Except for this brief contact with the living, the spirit world exists in perpetual darkness and emptiness, as in an unlit and unoccupied theatre:

> WE DO NOT SEE EACH OTHER, JUST THE LIT
> SPACE OF YR GLASS EACH TIME U ENTER IT (CL 152–53)

The interchange between the mortal and immortal comprises a play of its own which "IS WRITTEN AS WE SPEAK / . . .YR ENERGIES / MY FRIENDS ARE OUR AUDIENCE, THEATRE & SCRIPT" (CL 191). This is the play that every human has running within himself, the divine conversing with the mundane in an endless revival of that original production from millennia ago.

That original play, which myth repeats over and over again as variations on the song of destiny, is built into our bodily chemistry. It is represented by Merrill as being contained in the DNA molecule, which serves as prompter in our revival house, "a spiral molecule / Whose sparklings outmaneuver time, space, us" (CL 274). This spiral molecule is the staircase of destiny wedded to possibility, nature wedded to mind, which one mounts on the way to enlightenment. Our steps through the various trials by fire and tears of which our life is comprised trace the "gull's / Ascending aureole of decibels" (CL 274), from whose high vantage—the completed poem and successful initiation into the mysteries of being—all of creation comes into view as a text to be read, understood, and enjoyed:

> The message hardly needs decoding, so
> Sheer the text, so innocent and fleet
> These overlapping pandemonia:
> Birdlife, leafplay, rockface, waterglow
> Lending us their being, till the given
> Moment comes to render what we owe. (CL 275)

If the message that creation gives us needs no interpretation, it is because we are *of* the world as well as in it. When we look about us, we see "both a holy and a homely site" (CL 112). Mirabell's healing message to his initiates is that salvation from the absurd lies all around us, in the miracle of life, in mortality itself, which "ALLOWS FOR THE DIVINE TRANSLATION" (CL 200) by which matter is spiritualized and spirit is given material form. When mind and nature are wedded, when matter and myth are imbued with one another, the birds live, the leaves play, and the water glows.

The questers of *Ephraim*, whom we see facing the vision of the absurd at the end of that poem, metamorphose in this purgatorial volume into the initiates of Mirabell who are healed and purified by giving in to "THE DEEP DEMANDING IMPULSE TO LIFE" (CL 275), our sole refuge from the absurd, which is death.

5

Empty Perfection: *Scripts for the Pageant* and *The Higher Keys*

When one is writing about a poem in trilogy form, it is perhaps impossible to escape what Merrill refers to as "the tyrant Three" (CL 530): thesis, antithesis, and synthesis. We may console ourselves with the knowledge that the poet himself claims to have been bound by this "Ménage à trois" (CL 530) and will content ourselves in this chapter with an attempt to explain the manner in which the form is adhered to, and rebelled against, in *The Changing Light.*

In *The Book of Ephraim,* the working thesis is the Jungian assertion that "God and the Unconscious are one" (CL 74). Operating under this assumption, the poet embarks upon a quest to uncover the self's unconscious will, a quest to know the self and God. The quest is circular. Once the self and God (or the unconscious) are recognized as being equivalent, the self is forced to separate from the ubiquitous unconscious in order to save itself—the alternative is a "giving in" to the amoral and all-powerful unconscious, which leads to the vision of the absurd and, eventually, to a loss of the self's autonomous will, the inevitable result of which is death.

The doctrine espoused by the angels and their subordinates in *Mirabell* is set against the vision of the absurd that the poet-quester experiences at the conclusion to *Ephraim*. The quest in *Mirabell* is linear and teleological. The questers are figured as students, patients, and initiates, all of which implies that they are in a subordinate position to some higher figure of power. Progress is required before they can graduate into the elite group of which their mentors are members. The quest is other-centered, as opposed to the egocentric quest of *Ephraim*. The importance of the "other" is reinforced by the narrative form of the poem, which implies an audience and a story, both of which are placed in a superior position to the personality of the poet. He is the mere conduit of the story being dictated to him by his superiors.

The story or message that the poet receives and delivers in *Mirabell* is centered on the theme of interdependence: between man and his environment, mind and nature, poetry and science, ideas and images, and the individual talent and the tradition in which he or she works. The message is anti-individualist. History, heredity, science, culture, and society—the great givens—are the heroes of this poem.

In *Scripts for the Pageant*, the poet returns to the themes of *The Book of Ephraim* and abandons the themes of *Mirabell*. The spirits in this concluding volume praise individualism and question authority, urging JM to abandon the passive, "good student" attitude he adopts for *Mirabell*. The higher powers in *Scripts* are so contradictory in their teachings and undermine their own credibility to such an extent that the poet-quester feels forced to fall back upon his skeptical pre-*Mirabell* self, which remains the one constant upon which he may rely. In this volume, JM puts his faith, once again, in the "black magic" (CL 455) of human "feeling" and intuition (CL 426), allowing his "feminine" unconscious—banished in *Mirabell*—to reassert itself in the figures of Gabriel and Mother Nature, the most important characters to be introduced in this character-rich poem.

Gabriel is the most human of the four archangels present in this poem. Like us, he is subject to time and feeling. Time reemerges as the major theme of the trilogy, the theme that was "forbidden" and "forgotten" in *Mirabell* (CL 438). The quester of *Scripts*, unlike the quester of *Ephraim*, refuses to be drawn into the unwinnable, if heroic, struggle against time. In this concluding volume, the poet-quester seeks to make his peace with time so that he may reenter the "real" world.

The poet returns to his starting place in *Ephraim*, in which he feels forced by the constraints of time to choose between art and life, between the life that is recorded and saved, if only artificially, and the life that is fully *lived*. The quester of *Scripts* is an older and wiser quester, one who has learned the vanity of the human wish either to conquer or banish time. Although the consequences of choosing between life and art are real, the choice itself is not. This paradoxical knowledge that the quester has gained through his trials makes him at once more skeptical and more resigned than in *Ephraim*. Skepticism and resignation are the narrow poles between which the argument in this poem runs in a continual dialectic of yes and no. Pushed far enough, the passive attitudes of either skepticism or resignation may develop into a call for action. Working together, they serve to cancel each other out, resulting in neither skepticism nor resignation, but in a weary nostalgia.

We witness the dialectic between skepticism and resignation in the central passage of this poem, in which the poet returns to his theme of the fall into time as represented by his parents' divorce. In the poem based on this divorce, "The Broken Home," Merrill presents us with two versions of time. Time is figured as circular, represented by the archetypal feminine figure, the earth mother who is ruled by recurring seasons. Time is also linear, symbolized by the archetypal masculine figure, the sky father of creation myths, who represents a higher world of perfection, in which time, being endless—a straight line stretching out into infinity—has no ultimate meaning. *The Book of Ephraim* is dominated by the recurring (feminine) circular time pattern. Followed far enough, this leads to the vision of the absurd. *Mirabell* is dominated by the masculine and "Platonic" linear model, which implies a banishment of time.

In this crucial passage in *Scripts for the Pageant*, the poet argues that the "friction" between these two time patterns—circular and linear, feminine and masculine—results in life as we know it (CL 495). The poet-quester of this last volume wants to break out of this closed system, to reach back "past the flailing seed" of self that is caught between the opposing poles of the feminine unconscious and the masculine conscious. But he is stopped in his tracks by Maria's resigned admonition:

> HUSH ENFANT   FOR NO MAN'S MIND CAN REACH
> BEYOND THAT HIM & HER   THEIR SEPARATION
> REMAINS UNTHINKABLE.   WE ARE CONFINED
> BY THE PINK CARNATION, THE FERN FIDDLEHEAD
> & THESE BREATHMISTED PANES OF HUMAN SPEECH (CL 495–96)

We might take the pink, "flesh-colored" carnation to be a clever representation of the ever-ripe, feminine, libidinal self—the god of *Ephraim*—as the fern "fiddlehead" may be taken to represent, in a playful and satirical manner, the masculine, rational self that dominates in *Mirabell*. The fiddlehead fern's "spiral" form would also align it with the "DNA-dominated" self of *Mirabell*. Both the feminine and masculine selves are made manifest in speech.

The poet-quester of this passage feels imprisoned by these categories. Maria's insistence that the categories are unbreakable—"NO MAN'S MIND CAN REACH / BEYOND THAT HIM & HER"—fuels his feeling of skepticism in the face of helplessness. It also seems to prompt his return to the beginnings of his private myth (as recounted in "The Broken Home") in an attempt to find the exact point at which the category-creating schism occurred, the "divorce" between the unconscious and the conscious, the timeless and the time-bound. He wants to heal this rent:

> *That* was the summer my par—YR PARALLELS
> DIVERGE PRECISELY HERE   I from the I
> Who shook those bars, who burned to testify
> At the divorce. Scales flashing, bandage loosened,
> Pitiless gaze shining forth—ah cover it
> While time allows, in decent prejudice!
> Mine's for the happy ending. Weren't the endings
> Always happy in books? Barbarity
> To serve uncooked one's bloody tranche de vie . . .
> Later, if the hero couldn't smile,
> Reader and author could; one called it style.
> Poetic justice, if you like. A spell
> Which in mid-sentence, turning iron to sunlight—
>
> Where were we? SAFE AS YET IN THE IMMORTAL CELL (CL 496)

We are, each of us, imprisoned in the immortal "cell" of the time-bound self, whose bars—the "I from the I"—might be taken to be the bars both of self-consciousness and of time itself. The poet's reference to the original "trial" at which the divorce between the eternal and the mutable takes place (though they live together, nevertheless, in "parallel" estrangement within each of us, since "THEIR SEPARATION REMAINS UNTHINKABLE") reminds us of our "convict" status. We owe this time-bound world a debt, a death.

Why? How did we lose our innocence? This is the crucial question that the poet is attempting to answer throughout the epic. He struggles to regain his original innocence, the "IMMORTALITY" that is every mortal's wish (CL 314), by reconstructing "THE PRIMAL SCENE" (CL 323) in which the innocence was lost. By reconstructing this scene, he hopes to discover "whether innocence / Is lost to guilt or to experience," whether we are to blame for our "lost" condition or whether we are Time's (or God's, or Fate's) victims (CL 322). In *Ephraim*, the conclusion seems to be that experience—time itself—is the culprit and that we all are implicated in time's conspiracy. In *Mirabell*, the spirits imply that we fall as a result of sin, that innocence is lost only to guilt. In *Scripts*, the question is left "hanging." Even the archangel Michael, the ruling spirit of *Mirabell*, whose benevolent presence seems to guarantee God's innocence in that poem, is forced to admit in *this* poem that none can

"SHED LIGHT" upon this original schism, "THE SPLITTING OF THOSE HOARY DOGMAS" (CL 323) by which we have been made convicts in this world.

Despite Michael's and Maria's implicit warnings about the futility of the effort, the poet-quester of the long passage above seems to be on the verge of restarting the unwinnable quest to reach back "past" the primal scene in which time and timelessness, the conscious and the unconscious, were originally split. In addition to the obvious allusion to "blind" justice, the "scales flashing" represent the quester's calling forth of the "dragon" of the unconscious, the destructive anima, whose appearance marks the beginning of the quest cycle in *Ephraim* and in the lost novel. The "loosened" bandage may be taken to symbolize the failure of the spirits of *Mirabell* completely to "heal" the quester of his self-defeating urge to combat time, just as it represents the "injustice"—the no longer blind, but *partial* justice—of the quester's situation.

As the skeptical poet-quester of *Scripts* threatens to metamorphose into the hopeless romantic quester, who is present in embryo form within every skeptic's heart, resignation paradoxically reasserts itself, and the quester willingly covers the eyes that would meet the "pitiless gaze" of the dragon of the unconscious. To meet and hold this gaze, as JM learns in *Ephraim*, is to bring oneself face to face with the absurd. To avoid this, the poet of *Scripts* resigns himself to the forcibly "happy" ending, abandoning his hero, JM, in favor of the author, James Merrill, forcing art to give life its due.

Scripts for the Pageant details the journey from art to life (the inversion of Proust's journey) and the unmasking of the questing hero—JM—to reveal the poet beneath. This journey is in response to *The Book of Ephraim*, which traces the development of its reluctant author into his role of hero-quester. In *Ephraim*, JM admits that his poetic endeavor through the Ouija board is, in one sense at least, simply the putting on of a mask, the wearing of which allows him to face otherwise unfaceable truths about himself and his life (CL 30).

The theme of unmasking runs throughout *Mirabell* and *Scripts*. The purpose of this unmasking in *Scripts* is not, as in *Mirabell*, to reach the ideal, essential world upon which the real world of appearances is merely projected. Rather, the purpose is to prove—to use Wilde's phrasing (to which Merrill alludes in *Ephraim* (CL 30))—that "the truths of metaphysics are the truths of masks" (1078). The poet-quester accepts in *Scripts* that there are no essences to be reached through art. To quote Wilde further, "a truth in art is that whose contradictory is also true" (1078). The closest the artist may come to *the* truth is to show, through the unmasking of opposing truths, that the answer to any metaphysical question in art is both "yes" and "no." Does God exist? Yes and no. Are we responsible for our own existence? Yes and no. Is the poet-quester responsible for his revelation? Yes and no. Does art steal from life? Yes and no. Is the artist therefore culpable? Yes and no.

The unmasking in *Scripts* often involves the debunking of old authorities. When DJ asks about Mirabell's masque from the preceding volume, Auden responds, "THE ONLY MASQUE IN QUESTION / HID A BIRDBRAIN. HE OF COURSE HAD HAD / NOT THE FOGGIEST . . . / NO WONDER HE LIES ABASHED HEAD UNDER WING / LIKE A SWAN" (CL 287). Ephraim, whose authority is consistently undermined by Mirabell, gets similar, if more sympathetic, treatment: "Poor Ephraim, we've all dropped him, like a mask" (CL 292). In the coda, *The Higher Keys*, Ephraim is reestablished as an important figure when his hidden identity as the archangel Michael is revealed. This is one of several crucial cases of mistaken identity that are corrected in *Scripts* and its coda. They serve to reinforce the theme of the "truth of masks" by persuading us that opposing allegorical characters and contradictory truths are in fact one and the same.

Ephraim and Michael are similar in appearance at least, but they have represented opposing camps throughout the trilogy, with Ephraim standing for the feminine unconscious in *The Book of Ephraim* and Michael representing the masculine, rationalizing, and idealizing mind of *Mirabell*. The revelation that the two characters are versions of one another serves to erase the distinction between the rational masculine mind and the feminine unconscious, which the poet has so carefully traced throughout the poem. It gives us further proof that all opposing factions from the poem's mythology will be reassimilated, by the poem's conclusion, into the single figure of the poet himself.

We may think of the characters in *Scripts* as self-destructing or as coalescing into one assimilable whole, in order to release their god and creator, the poet character JM, back into life. So it is that Maria, the single most real and convincing character in the trilogy, reveals that, far from representing the idealized feminine, the mother-sister-bride of *Mirabell*, she is the very author of the opposing masculine ideal, Plato himself. More than any other character, she urges JM to finish the poem and to return to real life:

> It's moving so quickly, you'll be gone,
> Maman, before we know it! AH COME ON
> THE MOON IS WAXING FULL
> & WE DEAR ENFANTS ALSO FEEL ITS PULL (CL 429)

The "tug" of time is felt more strongly in this volume than in either of the previous two. In *Mirabell,* time as a theme is banished. In *Ephraim,* the very difficulty and compactness of the narrative, its "timeskip and gadabout" (CL 115), prevent the reader from fully experiencing the poem as an elegy for lost time. But in *Scripts,* we experience the deaths of characters whom we have gotten to know intimately throughout the poem. These inevitable and, finally, "willed" deaths help to give this volume its oddly elegiac tone. The tone is odd, because this poet is *not* primarily an elegiac poet, and his "irrepressible brightness / —So like life" (CL 416) continually wears through the poem's veneer of death and loss. The give and take between death and life to which the poet provides free rein in this volume—not allowing himself to repress life in favor of death, coupling "gloom" with "artifice" (CL 76) as in *Ephraim,* or favoring life over death as in *Mirabell,* in which time and death are banished—makes this poem the most "Merrillian" of the three. The poem's unashamedly divided and dual nature mirrors the poet's own acknowledged bent toward "dualism."

I have suggested that we think of Merrill's dualism in *Scripts for the Pageant* as being characterized by opposing attitudes of skepticism and resignation. I would go further and argue that the attitude of skepticism dominates in *The Book of Ephraim,* in which the poet-quester's repeated failure to conquer time and break out of the circular quest cycle results in an ever-deepening skepticism. By contrast, the attitude of resignation dominates in *Mirabell,* in which the quest to conquer time is forbidden. These differing attitudes are reflected in the opening words of the two poems. *Ephraim* begins, "Admittedly I err" (CL 3). This phrase apologizes and challenges at the same time. The poet is apparently still skeptical about the nature of what is being presented and is implicitly challenging the reader to do better, even as he apologizes for the failure of his own effort. The skeptical attitude of the poet-quester in *Ephraim* results in his resistance to the established order. We witness this resistance in the character of JM throughout *The Book of Ephraim* as he continually struggles against the revelation that Ephraim has in store for him, fearing that art will endanger life, as his devotion to Ephraim has gradually replaced his devotion to Maisie, DJ, and himself.

Mirabell begins, "Oh very well, then " (CL 97). We detect an air of exaggerated exasperation in this that seems to imply that the poet is not as unhappy with what is to follow as he might like us to believe.

There is a smugness in the poet's resignation, as though he knows something that we do not about the unnecessary nature of what is, nevertheless, to follow. The resignation of *Mirabell* implies an acceptance of the established order and of limitation in general. We see evidence of this acceptance reflected in the "good student" attitude of JM throughout *Mirabell,* in which he refers to himself and DJ as the "docile takers-in of seed. / No matter what tall tale our friends emit, / Lately—you've noticed?—we just swallow it" (CL 154).

The dialectic between this resistance to and acceptance of limitation is continual in *Scripts for the Pageant,* and it may be seen as the synthesis of the prevailing attitudes represented in the opening phrases of the preceding volumes. Throughout *Scripts,* we witness instances in which the opposing attitudes of skepticism and resignation serve to invalidate one another. Mother Nature seems to be on the side of resistance when she explains how her twin brother, God B, instructed her to make man into a resistant creature (CL 408). The Ouija board participants are likewise praised when they resist the gods' imperiousness, as when Auden says, "IF I MAY SAY SO, WE DO NOT WORK WELL TO ORDER," and is commended by the archangel Michael, "POET, YOU AND YOURS ARE FREE HOW LONG IT HAS TAKEN YOU TO MAKE YOUR CLAIM!" (CL 391).

But earlier in the volume, Wystan and Maria say that they are "NOT RESIGNED" to their supposed fate of returning to the elements and mean to "RESIST," insisting on immortality, "WHY NOT? SHOOT FOR THE MOON!" JM responds, "You must be teasing us," and he is answered, "ALAS TOO TRUE" (CL 315). The questers are also told that there will be no resistance in paradise, and that perfected man will

> SWIM & GLIDE,
> A SIMPLER, LESS WILFUL BEING. DULLER TOO?
> IF SO, IS THAT SHARP EDGE NOT WELL LOST
> WHICH HAS SO VARIOUSLY CUT AND COST? (CL 512)

This cosmological contradiction between acceptance and resistance is present at the very heart of matter, as "GK," the scientist in the Ouija board seminar group, explains:

> WE MUST ASSUME THAT GOOD
> MATTER RESISTS BAD, THAT MATTER'S VERY
> NATURE AND ORIGIN ARE THIS RESISTANCE. LORDS?
> GOD BIOLOGY—DID HIS DIMENSIONLESS
> BLANK ENERGY, UNMEASURABLE, COME
> FROM A TRIUMPH OVER, OR A COMPROMISE WITH,
> BLACK MATTER? AT THAT FLUNG-UP WINDOW I
> WAS STOPPED. (CL 397)

The dialectic between struggle and compromise with matter is analogous to the dialectic between a resistance to and an acceptance of the limitations of time. In this final poem, the poet-quester strives to accept the dialectic between acceptance and resistance without taking sides. In so doing, he seeks to negate the dialectic's movement, insisting on a *final* synthesis of these endless dialectical debates. He implicitly and repeatedly demands to know whether acceptance of or resistance to the established order—life as we know it—will enable him to transform his life, to either save or negate time. Again GK considers this question in "material" terms:

> MATTER: IS IT POSSIBLE, LORD GABRIEL,
> TO PUSH OUT THROUGH THAT WINDOW? OR IS THAT THE
> DEATH BEYOND DEATH, THE VAST SABLE EMPTY
> HALL OF THE GOD, YOUR MASTER? (CL 397)

Gabriel assures GK that he will explain this issue, but the issue is never finally resolved in this poem, as JM admits with a rhetorical question,

> The ambiguities . . .
> Resolve them? Wear them on a ring, like keys
> The heroine in James how seldom dares
> Use, on the last page, to open doors? (CL 399)

Any resolution or simplification of the ambiguities would be a lie. To argue that we should either resist or accept the limitations of our mutable lives would be to evade the question, to deny the dualistic nature of life itself, which is best expressed through paradox and contradiction. Once again, Oscar Wilde seems to speak for the poet of *Scripts* when he asserts that paradoxes, though half-truths, are the best to be had (43).

The paradoxical and contradictory nature of this poem is well represented in the ritual by which the questers sever relations with their Ouija-board companions, breaking a mirror into a stream of running water, symbolizing both resistance and acceptance at once (CL 364). The argument of the poem that leads up to this farewell proceeds by contradiction. Consider the way in which white and black come to symbolize first one principle and then its opposite. In *Ephraim*, white stars are opposed to black holes in space, as a printed black and white photograph is the opposite of its negative. In that volume, the poet seems to find reassurance in the knowledge that the darkness of the negative or of the black hole implies light, since darkness is, by definition, simply the absence of light. In *Scripts* JM attempts to assuage DJ's fears with this positive view of the dark: "from the darkness you foresee, / Who knows what may develop milkily, / What loving presence?" (CL 362). This reassurance, which in *Ephraim* serves to enhance the questers' natural inclination toward light and away from the dark, develops in *Scripts* into an actual preference for darkness over light.

When JM and DJ complain that the "RADIANT LIGHT" (CL 305) that is supposedly emanating from them into the other world is a light they cannot see, a light that they "are the two contracted pupils of," they are warned: "YET FOR THAT FOCAL DARKNESS THANK GOD B / MY BOYS IT IS YR PRECIOUS SANITY" (CL 306). Later in the poem, GK hypothesizes that the "WHITE OF MIND / UNLIMITED" is an amoral "WHITE REASON" (CL 447) that destroys the imagination and its metaphors, the black holes by which we evade unanswerable questions and the imponderable metaphysical questions that white reason would continually pose to us: Where did we come from? Where are we going? Why are we here?

These are the essential questions that the epic poet asks. In this third volume, Merrill questions the viability of such probing. We can sense the approaching conclusion of the poem in the poet's unwillingness to continue pressing himself for answers to what he now understands to be unanswerable queries. To escape further questioning, he takes "REFUGE" in the very "BLACK HOLE" (CL 447) that he so disparages at the beginning of his quest in *Ephraim* (CL 85)—the black hole of the unexamined and unwritten life and of the mundane world of mutable loves and losses—from whose vantage point the quest for revelation, "illumination's blindfold," glows only dimly "in recollection" (CL 515).

The black hole in this poem represents the mystery of existence, "mere being," which escapes all effort at artistic encapsulation:

> My characters, this motley alphabet,
> Engagingly evade the cul-de-sac,
> Of the Whole Point, dimensionless and black,
>
> While, deep in bulging notebooks, drawn by it,
> I skim lost heavens for that inky star. (CL 454)

From the other world's viewpoint, this star, whose "inky" negative we behold from our sublunar world, appears to be the brightest of lights: "IT'S LIKE A STAR WE ENTER / TO FIND OURSELVES. . . . THE LIGHT OF LOVE" (CL 499). This is the light that appears to us as a "blind spot. . . . the screen / Of self which forms between God and His creature" (CL 499).

Near the end of *Scripts* in a densely packed *terza rima* section set in Venice (recalling sections V and W of *Ephraim* and containing allusions to most of the poem's major themes), we are given an infernal and carnal version of the black hole of human nature. It is figured, in this instance, as the "glory hole" of a glass-blower's furnace:

> The street—
> At-evening's densely peopled Coromandel
>
> Panel folds back upon a blast of heat
> So powerful we've paused: it's the glass-blowing!
> A glory hole roars, pulses. Color of peat
>
> Artisans dip the long rod into glowing
> Pots, fire within fire, gasping conflate
> Ember with embryo, by rote foreknowing
>
> —Much as they twirl, lop, tweezer at a rate
> Swifter than eyesight—the small finished form.
> Twice more we watch the rose-hot blob translate
>
> Itself to souvenir, to hardly warm
> Bud-vase or pony, harlequin or bird—
> Its newfound cool no refuge from the storm
>
> Of types—and can move on. (CL 504)

The furnace of this passage recalls the broken furnace in the Stonington house at the end of *Ephraim* and the belching and grumbling "Greedy, / Erotic little orc" (CL 433) at the end of section "&" earlier in *Scripts*.

The pulsing "glory hole" that receives the "long rod" is blatantly sexual, but we would misinterpret this passage—and the symbolism of the furnace throughout the poem—were we to see it as *only* sexual. It is the furnace of making and of being, whose final, unfixable failure comes only with death. Its presence in the crowded center of town or in the "dark annex" (CL 433) of the house (symbols of the self) is felt continually, but it may be seen only in moments of revelation "so powerful we've paused." In these sublime moments, the self appears suspended in time, its past, present, and future condensed into the ritual moment. The ritual of the glass-blowing of this passage returns us to the pivotal passage at the end of section V, in which JM is turned symbolically into "a glass model of stamina" (CL 503) and embarks upon his epic quest either to save or to conquer time.

In this passage, the quester reviews his progress in the quest, the "translation" of the embryos into souvenirs, which recall the major symbols and characters of the poem. Bud-vase, pony, harlequin, and bird recall Rosamund Smith, Uni, Ephraim, and Mirabell. The quester has succeeded in creating the "conventional stock figures" (CL 4) that he claims to want at the beginning of the poem. Now he fears that the "storm of types" he has created in search of the universal in art has succeeded all too well. The generic of art has in fact replaced the specific in life, leaving the poet but one recourse—to move on:

"Happy ending?"

Smiles DJ as we link arms, tacitly
Skipping the futuristic coffee-bar's
Debate already under way (ah, me)

On the confusing terms: Dance, Gods, Time, Stars. (CL 506)

The poet's decision to break with the other world leaves him with mixed feelings, which are made evident in a beautiful passage concluding the "YES" section of the poem:

A SHIPBOARD SCENE,
TRISTAN ACT I OR LES TROYENS ACT V:
HIGH IN THE RIGGING, FROM
BEHIND THE GOLD PROSCENIUM
ABOVE THE ACTION'S THRIVING
CITY WITH ITS WRONGED & WILFUL QUEEN,

ONE SAILOR'S CLEAR
YOUNG TENOR FILLS THE HOUSE, HOMESICK, HEARTSICK.
THE MAST NEEDS COMFORT. GALES
HAVE TATTERED THE MOONBELLIED SAILS.
MAY HIS GREEN SHORES O QUICKLY
SAFELY NOW FROM RAGING FOAM APPEAR. (CL 365)

This passage is taken down by Merrill from Auden's Ouija-board dictation. There *are* Auden-esque qualities to these stanzas, particularly, to my ear, in the two concluding verses. But one would still not mistake it for Auden. We rather see in it an example of Merrill doing one of the things that he does best: setting a scene, and bringing that scene to life through a combination of vivid description, eccentric diction and syntax ("MOONBELLIED SAILS"), and an anthropomorphism that tends toward pathos ("THE MAST NEEDS COMFORT").

The dandified pathos of the passage is a typically Merrillian coupling in which we detect a sadomasochistic tendency, as in Swinburne or Proust, to punish a natural bent toward extravagance with a forcibly resigned or skeptical attitude. The presence of the queen who is both "WRONGED & WILFUL" serves to reinforce the feeling we have that the poet of the passage is torn between a forced resignation and a temperamental superciliousness.

The queen's presence would allow us to place this passage in the poem's third volume, had we not known where it belonged. In *Scripts*, the poet finally seems able to confront the archetypal feminine without flinching. In *Ephraim*, the poet-quester both despises and idealizes the feminine. In *Mirabell*, the feminine is actively negated. The poet of the above passage, however, is able to recognize the archetypal feminine as being both wronged and willful. The distance implied by this even-handed judgment insulates the poet from the effects, harmful and helpful, of the "Ewig-Weibliche" (Eternal Feminine). Having put the feminine in its place, the poet of *Scripts* is no longer in danger of being drawn into the feminine/unconscious-inspired quest that leads to the absurd. He has also cut himself off from his muse and must therefore face the inevitable conclusion of his poem as the "GREEN SHORES" of real life come into JM's "HOMESICK, HEARTSICK" view.

The homesick and heartsick feeling pervades this farewell poem. It is even felt by the ruling deity of the poet's pantheon, God B, whose cryptic message to the pantheon whence *he* comes is interpreted by JM as meaning: "*I've found work, we get on, Sister* [Nature] *keeps house. / Stay well, and please do not abandon us*" (CL 494). All of the gods of this poem are domesticated in this manner and appear as something *less* than human. The angels refer to the "CURSE OF IMMORTALITY" (CL 346). Gabriel and Mother Nature, the *most* human of the gods, are the gods who are least reduced by poem's end. The poet's depreciation of his cosmos works to reaffirm this poem's espousal of individual human nature as being, in its inconstancy, the one and only constant upon which it is safe to rely.

The return to human nature as the standard of value in this poem is mirrored by the poet's return to his original, pre-crisis, pre-Ephraim poetic nature. The poetic habits and traits that we have come to recognize as being most uniquely Merrill's are most apparent in this third volume of the trilogy. Auden may be understood to be defending Merrill's poetic mannerisms and excesses when he says:

> IS IT NOT OUR LESSON THAT WE COME
> EACH TO HIS NATURE? NOT TO ANY VAST
> UNIVERSAL ELEVATION, JUST
> EACH TO HIS NATURE PRECIOUS IF BANAL
> LIKE THE CLICHE UNCOVERED AMONG GEMWORDS (CL 308)

We detect Merrill's poetic nature in this volume's obsession with word-play and word-painting, as well as in his continual willingness to sacrifice truth to beauty, as he playfully and painfully takes apart the previous volumes' metaphysical and symbolic systems.

In place of these systems, we are given pageantry and camp. In *Scripts*, the idealized masque figures of *Mirabell* are exaggerated and, in the process, demythologized, to such an extent that they come to resemble the "imps of the anti-masque" (CL 263) more than they do their idealized selves. The elaborate poetics of *Mirabell*, which serve to illustrate the very nature of being, the divine wedding of idea to image and of mind to nature, metamorphose in this concluding volume into mere shop-talk and artistic backbiting. This is best illustrated by Auden's continual deprecation of the Archangel Michael's limited and outdated poetic practices.

Readers who prefer to think of this poem, and of this poet, as being in the great occultist/prophetic line of Blake and Yeats will most likely find *Scripts for the Pageant* more bothersomely frivolous than the previous two poems. By contrast, fans of Merrill's earlier work who are bewildered by these prophetic books may well find *Scripts* the least bewildering of the three. *Scripts* will appeal to those who are not interested in or attracted to prophetic poetry. It is more of a mock-epic than either *Ephraim* or *Mirabell*. The mock-epic element is certainly present in these earlier volumes, but it does not dominate as it does in *Scripts*, where the mock-epic spirit is appropriate to the movement of the poem's major argument: the displacing of art by life. In *Scripts*, we find the negation of the prophetic, psychoanalytic, and humanistic systems that have been elaborated in *Ephraim* and *Mirabell*, leaving the finished trilogy unencumbered by restricting dogmas and unbuttressed by belief.

One bit of dogma remains unrefuted—the belief that art and life are in opposition to one another and that a devotion to one necessitates a renunciation of the other. To illustrate the struggle between art and life, Merrill presents us in the coda with a reversal of Wilde's *The Picture of Dorian Gray*. In Merrill's rendering, the portrait, which is kept, as in Wilde's novel, in the upstairs "nursery" of childhood, is gradually effaced as its subject comes to life. The effacement of the portrait is the reversal of the poet's felt "self-effacement" in *The Book of Ephraim*—"Better to stop / While we still can. Already I take up / Less emotional space than a snowdrop" (CL 89)—and serves to illustrate the concluding poem's general theme of art returning to, or giving way to, life, as the poet prepares to abandon the poem and its characters:

> henceforth we'll be more and more alone.
> Uni, our Peacock, Ephraim—each of these
> We have by imperceptible degrees
> . . .What to say? Not tired of. Outgrown? (CL 540)

The subject of the portrait in the coda is Merrill's old Stonington friend, Robert Morse, whose death has been recorded earlier in the poem. Robert is being prepared to be reborn as "Tom." The name recalls the tragi-comic hero of the Stravinsky/Auden-Kallman opera, *The Rake's Progress*. In his new life, Robert is to be, appropriately enough, a composer whose task it is to design "A MUSIC TO / CLEAN UP & THIN OUT THE WESTERN SCENE" (CL 530). His music will accompany the birth of an alpha man, an "improved" and immortal human being who will no longer experience the "dualism" of our mutable existence. This perfected creature will have no need or knowledge of the resistance to death that impels our lives (CL 410). Robert's music is to embody "non-resistance" in its refusal to follow the conventional and seemingly inescapable "tyrant Three," a-b-a, which embodies resistance. "IT WILL BE A &1/2 CLEANSED OF FALSE DRAMA / A BOREDOM FALLING ON BORED EARS, RESOLVING / INTO A TASTE FOR LESS" (CL 530).

The fact that Merrill's version of paradise is characterized most forcibly by the boredom of its inhabitants would seem to indicate to us that this is not the paradise for him. As with Stevens in "Sunday Morning," Merrill envisions a paradise of pure perfection as the saddest of worlds, "With rivers like our own that seek for seas / They never find, the same receding shores / That never touch with inarticulate pang" (PEM 7). This predicted paradise is the remnant of the poem's elaborate mythology, most of which, by this point, near the conclusion of the poem, has already been discredited and discarded. Such a paradise makes us thankful for our resistant natures, even if this resistance is what chains us to the ever-repeating "tyrant Three": thesis, antithesis, synthesis: a-b-a.

Merrill's naming the reborn Robert after the laughable and pitiable Tom Rakewell indicates that he would rather be subject to the tyranny of resistance—implying the *existence* of both time and life, as well as death—than be a mere cog in necessity's endless mechanism. In Auden's opera libretto, Tom is "saved" from his bargain with Shadow, the representative of necessity in the opera, by his love for this mortal world, symbolized by his devotion to his beloved, Anne Truelove. His allegiance to "Truelove"—the idealized, allegorical symbol for the unconscious, libidinal self, the desiring self that never learns and is never sated but must be repeatedly assuaged—would indicate to us that he is able to make his destiny his choice. He chooses to be subject to his repetitive human nature, in which Truelove is won and lost repeatedly, rather than die the spiritual death that is the result of forsaking the ideal of Truelove altogether, thereby losing what is potentially the best and worst of human nature. Tom's devotion to his idealized past life and love enables him to escape necessity's grasp, though at the "price" of reason—for, with his escape from necessity, he also loses his sanity.

The devotion to an ideal comes at the price of the real. This has been Merrill's theme throughout the poem, and his use of *The Rake's Progress* and his allusions to *The Picture of Dorian Gray* in the coda simply serve to reinforce this theme of the incompatibility of art and life. We find no beatitude in these final sections of the trilogy. The ideal and the real fail to converge into one blessed whole. The poet's disappointment in his failure to achieve this vision of wholeness may be felt in the sentimentality of his conclusion. This sentimentality is the product of an agitated ambivalence.

Merrill's temperamental requirement that he be always "very, very intelligent" (DN 146) seems to insure that he will not allow himself the final extremes of asceticism and renunciation necessary for belief. Such asceticism need not be either "simplistic" or "naïve" (DN 147), but it must be willed, an active renunciation as opposed to passive resignation. The skeptical intelligence that would preclude the faith necessary for this poet to believe in his own vision serves to make this volume both frustrating and heartbreaking for the reader who has cheered the poet along his journey.

For all of this poem's celestial hierarchies, Merrill remains supremely a poet of earth. What attracts us to him is the very temperament that makes him, like Elizabeth Bishop, an unbeliever. He is sentimental in the old and positive sense of the word, valuing the feelings of ordinary existence above all else. The individual who puts his faith in feeling *is* skeptical, having experienced repeatedly the awesome tyranny of human emotion, its disappointing lapses and self-abusive obsessions. Merrill has that rare gift for the elevation of sentiment into great art that we find in Proust and in the Shakespeare of the late romances. Our quotidian loves and losses *are* sentimentalized and are best represented by that rare talent with the gift of sentiment evident in the trilogy's closing scenes.

> For affection's
> Poorest object, set in perfect light
> By happenstance, grows irreplaceable,
> And whether in time a room, or a romance,
> Fails us or redeems us will have followed
> As an extension of our "feel" for call them
> Immaterial, the real right angle,
> The golden section—grave proportions here,
> Here at the heart of structure, and alone
> surviving now to tell me where I am:
> In the old ballroom of the Broken Home. (CL 556–7)

Although Merrill fails to achieve a vision of paradise worthy of Dante, he succeeds in winning a transcendence comparable to Proust's. This transcendence is attained by the artist who creates a work of art as "reliquary" (CL 77), in which the "happenstance" moments of life when we intimate a *correspondence* between the mutable and the divine are preserved for posterity. Such an artist succeeds in making the present a home for the past, preserving in art what has been lost in living.

In these concluding volumes, we are admitted into the poem's making to a much greater extent than in the previous volumes. The poet's willingness to let stand the contradictory hierarchies and theories put forth by the spirits in *Scripts* serves as proof of his trust in us as readers and fellow pilgrims. The poet has let down his mask, or else, he has succeeded so successfully in creating a persona that he can go no further. In either case, the result is that we are put at ease and treated as equals. In *Scripts*, we reap the fruit of the lessons on manners in *Mirabell*. We have moved from the crisis management of *Ephraim*, to the schoolroom of *Mirabell*, and on to the "salon level" of *Scripts*. We have proven our worthiness as equals simply by having made it to this stage. Now we can relax and watch the pageant unfold before us.

A sense of playful artifice dominates in *Scripts*. It is present in the previous volumes and through all of Merrill's work, but never is it allowed free rein as it is here. Over-earnest readers are implicitly given their walking papers. They will only be offended by this poem's mockery of earnestness. We are all friends here, the poem seems to say, and friends do not impose upon one another with their earnestness. Art and life are successfully merged in this volume, in the sense that everyone present is operating on the salon level of idealized manners. This is a world in which everyone's destiny is his choice. Failure is something to laugh at or make fun of in good nature, as when Stravinsky "PROPOSES A NEW 'RAKE' / PROGRESSING THRU VARIOUS LIVES . . . ONLY / TO BE COMICALLY DEFEATED BY THE RATS" (CL 303). Later in the poem, a playful Mother Nature assumes the role of "Mother Goose," the brothel-keeper in Stravinsky's opera:

> NOW WHY DID I CHOOSE
> TO PLAY MOTHER GOOSE?
> FOR MAN MY HERO IS A RAKE! (CL 485)

The feminine Psyche-Nature figure is idealized in this poem as an indulgent and loving mother. She proclaims, "I AM ALL FOR MAN, YES, YES. / I LOVE HIM HELPLESSLY" (CL 409).

The vagaries of human nature are praised in this volume, even as they were criticized and condemned in the previous volumes. God himself is said to be "WISTFUL" of man's life (CL 463). When God B and his sister Psyche were creating man, they chose to "DIVIDE THE FORCE OF HIS NATURE. . . . / FOR IN DUALITY IS DIMENSION, TENSION, ALL THE TRUE GRANDEUR / WANTING IN A PERFECT THING" (CL 408). Perfection is boring. In this poem, the essence of perfection is subordinated to the appearance of human nature: "O IMAGES, DEAR ENFANT, IMAGES . . . / NEVER LET THOSE SCALES DROP FROM YOUR EYES" (CL 466). Plato is not the expounder of a hidden and higher world of forms in this poem. Rather, he too is enamored of appearances, "dropping" one charming young man in order to take up with another who is even more alluring. His fickleness prompts Auden to ask, "IS IT AS I ONCE WROTE, THAT GOD / JUDGES WHOLLY BY APPEARANCES?" (CL 291).

Psyche-Nature is representative of this volume in her obsession with good form. Mirabell tells JM and DJ that "NATURE IS THE MISTRESS OF THE ROBES MATTER / HER MATERIAL ITS CUT & STYLE, HER CEREMONY / WHO IS FOREVER CHANGING THE COSTUMES OF EARTH" (CL 288). *Her* costume is beyond reproach:

> *Enter—in a smart white summer dress,*
> *Ca. 1900, discreetly bustled,*
> *Trimmed if at all with a fluttering black bow;*
> *Black ribbon round her throat; a cameo;*
> *gloved but hatless, almost hurrying*
> *—At last! the chatelaine of Sandover—*
> *A woman instantly adorable.* (CL 407)

This is the "*third / And fairest face of Nature,*" Nature as Psyche (CL 407). Her other faces are the faces of chaos and of nature itself. It is accepted as inevitable in this poem that all of the characters are at least two-faced, if not three-faced. The fey and charming Ephraim is one of the faces of the imposing archangel Michael. Maria is one of the "faces" of Plato, an incorrigible cross-dresser. God B is both the ultimate ruler of this world and the much-put-upon younger brother in a divine pantheon.

For all of its playfulness, this is a very adult poem. It is adult in the manner of Pope's poetry. The poet is speaking to an elite and cultured audience, as one equal to another. The poem implicitly argues, "We can *act* like children because we know all too well that we are not. Why deny ourselves the consolation of playfulness, given the world we live in? This world, one hardly needs to say, is often most childish when it thinks itself most serious. By our play, we can both make fun of its childishness and console ourselves for having to put up with it."

The elitism of the poem is unrepentant and integral to its argument. Hierarchies are accepted as inevitable and even desirable. The Ouija-board salon/schoolroom, like any club, is desirable precisely because it is so hard to get into:

> SINCE LESSON I OUR SCHOOLROOM HAS BECOME
> A . . . CLOSED CIRCUIT NONE MAY PLUG INTO
> WITHOUT CREDENTIALS. IT IS BURKE'S NEW PEERAGE (CL 371)

After JM and DJ are allowed to hear God B's "song" to his brothers in the greater pantheon, Maria comments, "ENFANT ONE HATES TO BOAST BUT IT'S TOP DRAWER" (494).

Opposed to this self-satisfied elitist aura is the isolation of the privileged. God B, the most privileged character in the poem, is also the most isolated, singing into the abyss:

> BROTHERS HEAR ME BROTHERS SIGNAL ME
> ALONE IN MY NIGHT BROTHERS DO YOU WELL
> I AND MINE HOLD IT BACK BROTHERS I AND
> MINE SURVIVE BROTHERS HEAR ME SIGNAL ME
> DO YOU WELL I AND MINE HOLD IT BACK I
> ALONE IN MY NIGHT BROTHERS I AND MINE (CL 360)

DJ feels strangely akin to God B in his isolation, "It's almost as if we were dead / And signalling to dear ones in the world. . . . / We two are deaf and dumb; they see, they hear. / They suffer; we feel nothing. We're the dead" (CL 361). Eventually, the feeling of isolation so pervades the Ouija-board group that JM is led to admit, "*The manor is condemned. One doesn't dare / Say so flatly, but it's in the air*" (CL 482).

The poet and his Ouija-board companions are passengers on a celestial *Titanic*, celebrating as the ship goes down.

Like the mythical Titans, this poem's God B has been the victim of his progeny. He had "DREAMED OF CREATING A GOOD COMPANY AND A / FRIENDLY PLACE" (CL 293). But his first two creations were failures: "HE LONG KNEW THE FORCES ARRAYED AGAINST HIM: THE NEGATIVES, / THE VOIDS. HE HAD BEEN BESTED BEFORE" (CL 293). Man is God B's third and final child, as this poem is the third and final poem of the trilogy, and as Merrill himself was his father's third and final child and heir.

God B's three children are analogous to the three books of the trilogy. His first child had the shape of a winged man and the red eyes of Cain. He was rowdy and rebellious, a "SAD / MISTAKEN CHANGELING CHILD" who was allowed to die (CL 459). This first child was chaotic and difficult, like *The Book of Ephraim*. God B's second "horse-like" child was dependable and docile, like the well-mannered spirits of *Mirabell*. This second child "PROSPERED" and produced a creature of his own:

> 'GOD, FATHER, COME SEE WHAT I
> HAVE FASHIONED!'
> WE LOOKD INTO THOSE SELFSAME RED EYES. STRAIGHTENED.
> AND OUR FATHER SAID: I KNOW WHAT IS PAIN (CL 459)

The dependable second child, or poem, leads directly back to the chaotic first-born. We are stuck in the a-b-a trilogy prison. We have discussed the ways in which Merrill takes up the themes of *Ephraim* in *Scripts*. We might also draw a parallel between *Scripts* and God B's third child—man. Following this analogy, we symbolically break out of the a-b-a cycle, as man is prophesied to do when he becomes immortal (CL 530). Following this analogy, we can predict the conclusion of the poem just ahead. *Scripts* and its coda are the "A & 1/2," which stop the a-b-a cycle from repeating.

The "pageant" of the title implies a celebration of repetition wedded to progress. A pageant ritualizes both where we come from and who we are. The historical or mythical events depicted in the pageant are celebrated precisely because they have contributed to our own making and being. The pageant is directly opposed to the vision of the absurd, in which history is seen only as endless and fruitless repetition and in which identity is nullified. The pageant is a tribute to identity and to personality.

In *Mirabell*, the questers seek to know the essence upon which appearance is based. That volume's obsession with science, numbers, and ratios goes hand-in-hand with its devaluation of personality. In *Scripts* and its coda, personality is seen as crucial to being, even in heaven:

> STRANGE: 'PERSONALITY' I SHOULD
> HAVE THOUGHT THE CALLUS OF THE SOUL. NOT TRUE.
> A CERTAIN STRIDENCY MAY BE OUTGROWN
> SAY IN LISZT, BUT HIS ESSENTIAL HOKUM
> & GALLANTRY & ALL THE REST WD SEEM
> A CORE IMPERVIOUS TO THE PUMICE STONE (CL 527)

This observation is made by Robert Morse, the friend of the poet's who dies during the writing of the poem and is included in its making. His own personality, "self-effacing, witty, kind," ensures him a place at the Ouija-board table (CL 383). Personality is the unit of measure in heaven and in this poem. Robert has the wise, humble, and humorous "nature that in heaven opens doors":

> Tanya Blixen wants to dress him in
> Satin knee-britches—she his Marshallin?
> Colette abandons—Bernhardt takes to—bed.
> Alone, Jane Austen tilts but keeps her head,
> Addressing him, after a moment's droll
> Quiet of gray eyes beneath a parasol,
> as *Mr Robert*—a shrewd estimate. (CL 383)

Robert is perfectly fit to be taken up into this paradise of intelligence, wit, and taste. This poem envisions paradise as an elite social club in which the most sought-after invitation is the invitation to converse with the poet on the Ouija board. A running joke throughout the poem is the recently dead Vladimir Nabokov's rebuffed efforts to gain admittance to the board:

> Mr. Nabokov!
> Too embarrassing—again you've caught us
> With hands full. Would next month be time enough?
> GONE MES CHERS IN A HANDSOME (HORSEDRAWN) HUFF. (CL 526)

One wonders what behavior in real life led to such spurning in heaven. Nabokov's personality is perhaps too aggressive and competitive to earn him entrance into this world, in which making a fool of one's self is seen as preferable to making fools of others.

We admire the poet of *Scripts* for his willingness to play the fool. In some ways, this is a very silly poem, by its own admission and intention. It is silly in the manner of E. F. Benson and Ronald Firbank. This is the silliness of an elite that is *privileged* to be silly. One recompense for being "very, very intelligent" is that, among one's equals, where intelligence is a given, a very good time can be had by all. But there is more to "playing the fool" than simply being silly, as Auden points out when JM laments "Alone, I'm such a fool!"

> YES PARSIFAL, IN ONE SENSE I AGREE
> U'VE ON YR SIDE UTTER NEUTRALITY,
> NO MADE TO ORDER PREJUDICES NO
> BACKTALK JUST THE LISTENERS PURE O!
> NULL ZERO CRYING OUT TO BE FILLED IN:
> FOR ALL TOO SOON CONFRERE U MUST BEGIN
> TO JUDGE TO WEIGH WHAT'S CAST INTO THE SCALES (CL 328)

But does the holy fool ever truly judge? Is it not his talent simply to receive and, by his very lack of judgment, to stand for all of us?

One frustration with this poem stems from the discrepancy between the vision the poet says he desires and the vision he is willing to accept. JM is ambivalent in the face of revelation.

> ONE'S NOT MY BOY BRUSHED BY SUCH WINGS TO BE
> STILL OF TWO MINDS Deep down, you know I'm not
> —Or am I? Change the subject! (CL 399)

JM resists the spirits' pressure to make him take charge of the proceedings. Or does he? Who, after all, is *left* when the poem is finished? The spirits by this point have all self-destructed or coalesced. The poet's ambivalence is his strength, given the ever-shifting ground he stands on. He is resilient because he is amenable. An earnest, single-minded pilgrim would not survive in this topsy-turvy paradise.

Some readers may find that this poem speaks for their vision of existence, but most, I suspect, will not. Of the three poems, *Scripts* is the most personal and the least universal. What is personal about the poem is not the poet's life history, as in *Ephraim*, to which we can all relate, having histories of our own. Rather, we are given in this poem a 250-page metaphor of the poet's working mind and temperament. Nothing is less universal than temperament. This poem is a paean to an individual personality.

We can look on and marvel at the creative mind that could create such an elaborate metaphor. Nevertheless, unless we are "like-minded," we will not feel that this is our *story*, as *Mirabell* strives to be our story in its striving after the essence behind appearance. This is rather the story of a particular personality in a particular milieu, and it is this milieu, strange as it may be, that is being honored and preserved here. As in Proust, only the author and his friends are "saved" at work's end. This brings us back to our original contention that Merrill is not a public poet but a poet absorbed in the inner adventure of the private life.

Throughout his career, Merrill has striven to create a world in and through poetry to replace and pay tribute to the lost world of existence. Particularly he has striven to make up for his childlessness by creating an ideal family in art to replace the family he will not produce and the family in which he is still a child. In no other poem has he so successfully created an alternative family and world as in the conclusion to the trilogy. The reader is included in this close-knit world of the ideal family. This inclusion makes us feel that we too have something to lose when this poem is completed.

We can best characterize this poem and its world by describing the poet's temperament. This temperament:

> accepts failure as inevitable;
> is resigned, but not renunciatory;
> sings in its sadness;
> is surprisingly tough-minded;
> believes that "play" is valuable, as it diverts the mind from the unalterable and the inevitable;
> distrusts earnestness as leading to disappointment and unnecessary exasperation of sadness;
> is skeptical but not cynical;
> is gay-campy;
> is enamored of artifice;
> believes in form for form's sake;
> distrusts the overly intellectual;
> believes in the fundamental fallibility of human nature; and
> values consolation as the best and only remedy to loss.

This poem provides consolation for poet and reader. The ideal world of *Mirabell* is dismantled here as one would dismantle a bomb, because it is destined to lead us to grief. *Scripts* is the most Proustian of Merrill's poems in its dual effort to create a world and to destroy it. The skeptic in Proust and Merrill would convince us that this world was never real in the first place. We know better, and so do the creators. When reading or writing, we have *experienced* these worlds. The reader's and writer's act of sympathetic imagination is a mode of being. Being does not lie because it does not assert; it simply is.

The poem is a place of rest for life-weary souls. It is "made up," but so is life. The poem has the advantage over life of being finished and perfected. Life is a poor copy of art, as Wilde tells us. This poem concludes with a vision of art coming to the rescue of life, upbraiding existence for its imaginative poverty. This spirits have asked JM for a complete reading of his finished poem. Everyone who is anyone in the world of letters will be there—"MISS AUSTEN . . . CONGREVE & COLETTE / . . . . MARVELL & MALLARME" (CL 546–47), together with the Ouija-board spirits—and DJ and JM on *this* side of the mirror separating life from art.

They are all in place, and JM is set to begin "when shatteringly / The doorbell rings. Our doorbell here in Athens" (CL 558). Their friend Vasíli, whose wife Mimí has recently died, is at the front door,

> a form
> Gaunt, bespectacled, begrimed, in black,
> But black worn days, nights, journeyed, sweated in—
> . . . Ah sweet Heaven sit him down,
> . . . .
> He can't eat, can't sleep,
> Can't weep. D makes to put away the Board,
> Explaining with a grimace of pure shame
> —Because just as this life takes precedence
> Over the next one, so does live despair
> Over a poem or a parlor game—
> Explaining what our friend has come in on. (CL 558)

They offer their distraught guest sleeping pills, but he refuses and

> asks instead,
> Anything, *anything* to keep his head
> Above the sucking waves, merely to listen
> A little while. So in the hopelessness
> Of more directly helping we resume.
> Out come cup, notebook, the green-glowing room,
> And my worst fear—that, written for the dead,
> This poem leave a living reader cold—
> But there's no turning back.
> . . . .
> Both rooms are waiting.
> DJ brighteyed (but look how wrinkled) lends
> His copy of the score to our poor friend's
> Somber regard—captive like Gulliver
> Or like the mortal in an elfin court
> Pining for wife and cottage on this shore
> Beyond whose depthless dazzle he can't see.
> For *their* ears I begin: "Admittedly . . ." (CL 559–60)

This poem may have been written for the dead, but it is destined to be read by those in need of the consolation it has to offer to the living. Like all exiles, we are desperate for news from home.

Few poets in any generation feel the necessity or have the strength to "put it all down." The epic poet strives to see existence as a continuous whole. The lyric poet is content with parts of the whole. The epic poet in our time is faced with having to address an audience without a common mythology or system of belief. In the first volume of his trilogy, Merrill adopts Freud's and Jung's conception of the unconscious as the most credible modern metaphor for the mythic underworld. The quest in this volume is figured as the quest for psychic individuation. In the second volume of the trilogy, the poet uses the metaphor of scientific exploration into the nature of matter to represent the purgatorial quest for the refinement of the spirit. The quest in this volume is presented as a series of experiments and discoveries that gradually lead to enlightenment.

Neither psychology nor science is equal to representing a vision of paradise. In the third volume, the poet relies upon his unique imaginative temperament to give shape to revelation. While the paradise this poem envisions is not for everyone, we can all admire the faith necessary to bring it into being. Its creation was an act of devotion rare in an age of unbelief; its existence is an inspiration.

6

To All, Sweet Dreams: Concluding the Quest

The final and complete version of *The Changing Light at Sandover* was published in 1982. Between its publication and his death in 1995, Merrill published three more collections of poems. All three are strong volumes. Merrill's gift for translating life into art never deserted him after he reached his mature voice in his third volume, *Water Street*, in 1962. Merrill's final three volumes are the work of a proven major poet whose greatest achievement is behind him and of a temperament that is all too familiar with its strengths and limitations. The books are dominated by a backward look: rueful, forgiving, humorous, and knowing. In a sense, these final books form Merrill's *opus posthumous*, having been written on "the other side" of the epic that, one predicts, will form the basis of his enduring reputation.

In our study, we have traced Merrill's epic tendencies to his earliest poems and shown how they lead directly, and perhaps inevitably, to a masterpiece like *The Changing Light*. One poem in particular in Merrill's final volumes compels our interest. In "Nine Lives," the poet returns for a last visit to the house in Athens from whence emerged the Ouija-board epic. In the course of his stay, he is drawn back into the lost world of that epic only to be once again disappointed by its final dislocation from our quotidian lives. During the course of this valedictory sojourn, he is able to make his peace with that disappointment and, in so doing, put the final glaze upon his epic creation.

Let us begin with the poem's title. Like Dante, Merrill is obsessed with the figure of nine, which, being three squared, contains within itself both the three points necessary to form a circle, and the two points necessary to form a line. Nine is thus a numerical analog to the spiral, which results from the combining of the linear and the circular; it implies both progression and repetition or recurrence. The title, "Nine Lives," can be read in two ways, depending on whether we consider the second word to be a noun or a verb. It is an appropriately resonant title for a poem in which the life the poet lives is repeated, but at a distance, the space of years between abandoning the house in Athens and reinhabiting it.

The Athens house, possessed for so many years by JM and DJ, now appears to possess them, prompting the revival of thoughts and habits originally "fostered by the scene" (SS 6). This poem celebrates the house as ritual space and recalls Auden's late domestic sequence, "Thanksgiving for a Habitat," inspired by his farmhouse in Austria. As JM and DJ reenter the familiar house, JM instinctively inhabits the first floor: "*You* take the upstairs. These / Half-buried rooms, so glimmeringly tiled— / . . . keep me here, beguiled" (SS 5). His presence at the beginning of the poem in the darkened basement rooms recalls his previous inhabitings of the darkened living room at the beginning of "The Will" (SP 271) and of the "floor below" in the introduction to "The Broken Home" (SP 109). This poem will follow the pattern set by those earlier versions of the myth of deliverance, in which a crisis occurs, knowledge is earned, and peace is dearly bought.

"Nine Lives" is the last of the long series of poems that we have traced in the course of this study in which the poet interprets experience as a quest for the sublime. Not since the failure of that quest in *The Book of Ephraim* has the poet been willing to reengage his "period machine" (CL 91) in such a hopeful and hopeless task. In *Mirabell*, the quest is limited by the "NO ACCIDENT" (CL 179) clause, and in *Scripts*, the revelation of an intensely personal and private paradise takes precedence over earnest seeking. With "Nine Lives," Merrill returns us to his original theme enlarged upon in *Ephraim*: the struggle to wrest art from life and the debt to life the artist incurs in doing so. The poet's moral imagination, which admits of culpability and imperfection, is once again in control of his creation, having supplanted the aesthetic will to perfection that dominates in *Mirabell* and *Scripts*.

There are three major story lines in the poem; their obviousness is in inverse relation to their importance. The poem purports to be about the meeting set for 1991 (CL 509) of JM, DJ, and Maria's latest incarnation as an "Indian boy," whose heavenly task on earth it will be to discover a "POLLUTION-EATING ANTIGAS" (CL 419). JM and DJ are reminded of the meeting when they contact Ephraim on the Ouija board. They are given instructions as to the time and place of the meeting, and whom to look for. But the meeting fizzles as Ephraim fails to produce the Indian boy he has promised, whose appearance would have been the proof that the poet had "never had / Or asked for" (SS 8).

The second story line involves a family of cats that lives a precarious half-stray existence in the courtyard of the Athens house. The childless JM and DJ adopt the cats as their "latest Holy Family" (SS 8). JM proceeds to become attached to one kitten in particular. But the kitten's sensibilities as a stray will not allow of its being touched. When JM attempts to do so, the kitten "somersaults" in a panic off the three foot ledge that separates the courtyard of JM's house from that of the house below and then hides beneath an "oil drum / Mounted on venerable two-by-fours" (SS 9), refusing to be lured out. JM's foiled attempts to catch and rescue the kitten are pure slapstick comedy.

The comedy is a foil for the tragedy of the failed quest for the sublime, represented in this poem by the failure of Ephraim to produce "that child whose nature" would have "Proved Earth one with Heaven" (SS 15). The kitten's recurrent and resilient "nine life" nature is both reproof and reprieve from the vainglorious attempt to engender the "word made flesh" (SS 15). Unlike the imaginary Indian boy—the poem's false representative of revelation—the kitten is reliable, managing to work his way back up to JM's courtyard, and his nursing mother, via a makeshift bridge constructed by DJ and JM:

> We've propped the rough hypotenuse of board
> Between the pit to which his fall consigned
> Our prodigal and the haven left behind.
> Nature must do the rest. No coaxing toward
> The haggard matriarch on high. A blind
> Protecting us, we smile down through the slats
> As our flyblown road company of *Cats*
>
> Concludes its run. (SS 16)

The "rough hypotenuse of board" is, of course, the Ouija board, by means of which this prodigal poet son proves his devotion both to the the ideal of the h(e)aven left behind and to "the haggard matriarch on high," Mother Nature, that "ancient, ageless woman of the world" whom "the stars" wind each night "in filigree" (CL 92).

The "blind" that protects the poet from the absolute of the sublime is the "crucial blindness," the black holes discussed in *Scripts*, representing his irradicable human nature. In this poem, JM is reminded once again that the proof of divinity is both in him and of him, as well as all about him. It is the miracle whereby matter is imbued with spirit and spirit with matter; it is, finally, life itself, represented here by the unvanquishable kitten.

The third and crucial story line in the poem is the implicit story of the poet's renewed devotion to the "haggard matriarch" who is his muse and his mother, and the mother of us all. This feminine principle is travestied and, finally, abandoned in the concluding book of the trilogy. Her reappearance in this poem is proof of the poet's continuing devotion to experience, of his willingness to say yes again to life and love, proving that devotion through the conception and rearing of his progeny, art.

The willingness to say yes comes at a cost, as we discovered in our discussion of *The Book of Ephraim*, to which "Nine Lives" is clearly analogous. Both poems are concerned with the guilt and responsibility entailed by the parent, even of creative works. In this poem, JM's responsibility and guilt increase as he strives to capture the poem's legitimate—because real—symbol of the sublime, the prodigal kitten, consigned to the "pit" of the courtyard below by JM's original attempts at entrapment.

> With nimbleness approaching the sublime,
> Seizing a bathtowel against fangs and claws
> And lunging like an avatar of Shaw's
> Life Force, I overtook my prey in time
> To see him scuttle—not the slightest pause
> Or pity for one instant laughingstock—
> Into a vine-wreathed hole I'd failed to block.
>
> The roof next door is level with our own.
> It's there, as in a déjà-vu, mater-
> ialized a mother dolefully—night was near—
> Mewing down the drainpipe-telephone.
> Feeling our eyes, "Now just see what you've done!"
> Hers shone back. Such communicable pain!
> From being human we grow inhumane. (SS 10)

This is Merrill's most condensed, and perhaps most clever, version of the inevitable failure of the quest for the sublime. In two brief stanzas, he demonstrates how the human nature that is our glory is also our shame, as we strive for what we cannot have, strewing casualties in our path.

Here the masculine aggression of the poet-quester is rightly reproved by the feminine figure of the *mater dolorosa*. Later in the poem, the poet claims that the seeming abandonment of the rhyme scheme in line 2 of the second stanza above is an unconscious "lapse" (SS 16)—it is only after going onto the next line that we find that we have unwittingly mispronounced "mater." If it is a lapse, then it is a fortunate fall. By the reference to the mater-mother, the poet subconsciously prepares the way for his reacquaintance with the forgiving and consoling feminine principle from which he is estranged by his act of aggression against the natural order in seeking to capture the sublime.

In the next stanza, the poet admits his culpability in relation to the feminine mother figure and recalls his similar culpability in relation to his former lover, Strato:

> We have, it seems, methodically wrecked
> Her world. Analogies are rife and various
> To worlds like Strato's, now disaster areas
> We helped create. Hopeless to resurrect
> Cradles of original neglect. (SS 10)

Some sins are never forgiven. The guilt we entail in living, in choosing to abandon our original home and to live with one person over another, we carry with us throughout our lives. Fortunately, life provides us with myriad opportunities to atone for the guilt nursed in "cradles of original neglect."

In this poem, as in *Ephraim,* the poet's devotion to another and to an ideal removes from him the unendurable burden of guilt accumulated through living. By assuming responsibility for the kitten and admitting responsibility to others, including his old lover and, inevitably in this mother-dominated poem, his own mother, JM is able to redevote himself to his art with a clean conscience.

> To all, sweet dreams. The teacup-stirring eddy
> Is spent. We've dropped our masks, renewed our vows
> To letters, to the lives that letters house,
> Houses they shutter, streets they shade. Already
> Empty and dark, this street is. Dusty boughs
> Sleep in a pool of vigilance so bright
> An old tom skirts it. The world's his tonight. (SS 17)

The moon's pool of vigilance reminds us of the insistently fickle nature of our sublunar existence, from which the poet protects himself by withdrawing into his shuttered and shaded house of letters. If, like the old tom, he chooses to "skirt" the light rather than be blinded by it, this simply proves his devotion to the chiaroscurist nature of life itself.

The moon in this passage recalls the conclusion of the earliest poem in which Merrill called upon his Ouija-board experiences for inspiration. In that poem, written more than thirty years before the poem at hand, he contends that his commitment to the spirit world is not, as it might seem, a withdrawal from the real world, but an expansion of it: "Our lives have never seemed more full, more real, / Nor the full moon more quick to chill" (SP 48). The final line reminds us that no devotion is without risk.

This poet earns our own devotion by his repeated willingness to take the risks of creation, to give himself as fully as any poet in this century to the inspired madness of the artist, who knows all too well what such devotion requires of him in terms of self-sacrifice. In one of his most inspired conceits, Merrill in his last volume again utilizes the resonant image of the moon. In his conclusion to "Family Week at Oracle Ranch," the poet, after having dutifully completed an initiation into a "twelve-step program" of psychic healing (SS 80), considers the possibility, perhaps the inevitability, of a return to self-destructive habits.

> And if the old patterns recur?
> Ask how the co-dependent moon, another night,
> Feels when the light drains wholly from her face.
> Ask what that cold comfort means to her. (SS 80)

We find reassurance in a voice that refuses either to underestimate the pathos of our condition or to wish that it were otherwise. The cold eye that this poet casts on existence manages, through the strength of its vision, to console us with the truth.

Works Cited

Ashbery, John. *Selected Poems*. New York: Penguin, 1985.

Auden, W. H. *Collected Poems*. Ed. Edward Mendelson. New York: Vintage, 1976.

———. and Chester Kallman. Libretto. *The Rake's Progress*. Music by Igor Stravinsky. Cond. Riccardo Chailly. London Sinfonietta and Chorus. London, 411644–2, 1984.

Bachelard, Gaston. *Air and Dreams: An Essay on Imagination And Movement*. Trans. Edith Farrell and Frederick Farrell. Dallas: Dallas Institute Publications, 1988.

———. *Le Nouvel Esprit Scientifique*. Paris: Presses Universitaires de France, 1973. 5–17. Rpt. by Mary McAllester Jones in *Gaston Bachelard: Subversive Humanist*. Madison: University of Wisconsin Press, 1991.

———. *Water and Dreams: An Essay on the Imagination of Water*. Trans. Edith Farrell. Dallas: Dallas Institute Publications, 1983.

Bishop, Elizabeth. *The Complete Poems*. New York: Farrar Straus Giroux, 1979.

———. *One Art: Letters*. Ed. Robert Giroux. New York: Farrar Straus Giroux, 1994.

Blake, William. *Complete Writings*. Ed. Geoffrey Keynes. London: Oxford University Press, 1969.

Bloom, Harold. "The Internalization of Quest-Romance." *Yale Review* 58:4 (Summer 1969). In *Romanticism and Consciousness*, ed. Harold Bloom, 3–23. New York: Norton, 1970.

———. "Introduction." *James Merrill: Modern Critical Views*. Ed. Harold Bloom. New York: Chelsea House, 1985.

Carroll, Lewis. *Alice's Adventures in Wonderland*. New York: Signet, 1960.

Dante Alighieri. *Purgatorio*. Trans. Allen Mandelbaum. New York: Bantam, 1982.

de Grummond, Nancy Thompson. "Giorgione's 'Tempest': The Legend of St. Theodore," *L'Arte* 5, 19–19/20, 5–53.

Dickey, James. *Babel to Byzantium*. New York: Farrar Straus Giroux, 1968.

Eliot, T. S. *The Complete Poems and Plays*. New York: Harcourt, 1971.

Firbank, Ronald. *The Flower Beneath the Foot*. New York: New Directions, 1962.

Freud, Sigmund. *The Ego and the Id*. Trans. Joan Riviere, rev. and ed. James Strachey. New York: Norton, 1960.

———. *The Freud Reader*. Ed. Peter Gay. New York: Norton, 1989.
———. *General Psychological Theory*. New York: Macmillan, 1963.
———. *New Introductory Lectures on Psycho-Analysis*. Trans. and ed. James Strachey. New York: Norton, 1965.
Frye, Northrop. *The Myth of Deliverance*. Toronto: University of Toronto P, 1983.
———. *The Secular Scripture*. Cambridge, MA: Harvard University Press, 1976.
Howard, Richard. *Alone with America*. New York: Atheneum, 1980.
Jacoff, Rachel. "Merrill and Dante." *James Merrill: Essays in Criticism*. Ed. David Lehman and Charles Berger. Ithaca: Cornell UP, 1983. 145–158.
Jung, C. G. *Alchemical Studies*. Trans. R. F. C. Hull. Princeton: Princeton UP, 1967.
———. *The Psychology of the Transference*. Trans. R. F. C. Hull. Princeton: Princeton UP, 1966.
Keats, John. *The Complete Poems*. Ed. John Barnard. London: Penguin, 1973.
Mendelson, Edward. *Early Auden*. New York: Viking, 1981.
Merrill, James. *The Changing Light at Sandover*. New York: Knopf, 1993.
———. *The (Diblos) Notebook*. New York: Atheneum, 1975.
———. *From The First Nine*. New York: Atheneum, 1981.
———. "James Merrill." Personal interview with Thomas Bolt. In *Bomb* 36 (Summer 1991): 38–42.
———. *Late Settings*. New York: Atheneum, 1985.
———. *Recitative*. Berkely, CA: North Point, 1986.
———. *A Scattering of Salts*. New York: Knopf, 1995.
———. *Selected Poems*. New York: Knopf, 1993.
———. *The Seraglio*. New York: Atheneum, 1987.
Orgel, Stephen. *The Jonsonian Masque*. Cambridge: Harvard University Press, 1965.
Plato. *Apology, Crito, Phaedo, Symposium, Republic*. Trans. B. Jowett, Ed. Louise Ropes Loomis. Roslyn, NY: Walter J. Black, 1942.
Schikaneder, Emanuel. Libretto. *Die Zauberflöte*. Music by Wolfgang Amadeus Mozart. Cond. Neville Marriner. Academy of St. Martin in the Fields. Philips, 426 276–2, 1990.
Shakespeare, William. *A Midsummer Night's Dream*. Ed. Harold F. Brooks. London: Methuen, 1979.
———. *Complete Sonnets and Poems*. New York: Airmont, 1966.
———. *The Tempest*. Ed. Robert Langbaum. New York: Signet, 1964.
Stevens, Wallace. *The Necessary Angel*. New York: Vintage, 1942.
———. *The Palm at the End of the Mind*. Ed. Holly Stevens. New York: Vintage, 1967.
Trilling, Lionel. *E. M. Forster*. New York: HarBrace, 1967.
Wagner, Richard. *Götterdämmerung*. Cond. Georg Solti. Vienna Philharmonic and Chorus. London, 414 115–2, 1965.
———. *Die Walküre*. Cond. Wilhelm Furtwängler. Vienna Philharmonic and Chorus. Angel-EMI, CHS 7 630452, 1954.
Wilde, Oscar. *The Complete Works*. London: Collins, 1948.
Yeats, W. B. *The Poems of W. B. Yeats*. New York: Macmillan, 1983.
———. *A Vision*. New York: Macmillan, 1937.
Yenser, Stephen. *The Consuming Myth*. Cambridge: Harvard University Press, 1987.

Index

About the Author

DON ADAMS is Assistant Professor of English at Florida Atlantic University.

ISBN 0-313-30250-2
90000>
EAN
9 780313 302503
HARDCOVER BAR CODE